60¢   5

Controversies in Sociology
edited by
Professor T. B. Bottomore and
Professor M. J. Mulkay

16
The Limits of Rationality

Controversies in Sociology

1 SOCIAL THEORY AND POLITICAL PRACTICE
by Brian Fay

2 UNDERSTANDING SOCIAL LIFE
by William Outhwaite

3 SOCIALISM: THE ACTIVE UTOPIA
by Zygmunt Bauman

4 DILEMMAS OF DISCOURSE
Controversies about the Sociological Interpretation of Language
by Anthony Wootton

5 SOCIAL EVOLUTION AND SOCIOLOGICAL
CATEGORIES
by Paul Q. Hirst

6 THE LIBERATION OF WOMEN
A Study of Patriarchy and Capitalism
by Roberta Hamilton

7 MARX AND THE END OF ORIENTALISM
by Bryan S. Turner

8 SCIENCE AND THE SOCIOLOGY OF KNOWLEDGE
by Michael Mulkay

9 INTELLECTUALS AND POLITICS
by Robert J. Brym

10 SOCIOLOGY AND HISTORY
by Peter Burke

11 A THIRD WORLD PROLETARIAT?
by Peter Lloyd

12 MAX WEBER AND KARL MARX
by Karl Löwith
Edited and with an Introduction by Tom Bottomore and William
Outhwaite

13 POSITIVISM AND SOCIOLOGY: EXPLAINING SOCIAL
LIFE
by Peter Halfpenny

14 AESTHETICS AND THE SOCIOLOGY OF ART
by Janet Wolff

15 CAPITAL, LABOUR AND THE MIDDLE CLASSES
by Nicholas Abercrombie and John Urry

The Limits of Rationality
An Essay on the Social and Moral Thought of Max Weber

ROGERS BRUBAKER
Paul F. Lazarsfeld Fellow, Columbia University

London
GEORGE ALLEN & UNWIN

Boston   Sydney

George Allen & Unwin (Publishers) Ltd,
40 Museum Street, London WC1A 1LU, UK

George Allen & Unwin (Publishers) Ltd,
Park Lane, Hemel Hempstead, Herts HP2 4TE, UK

Allen & Unwin, Inc.,
Fifty Cross Street, Winchester, Mass. 01890, USA

George Allen & Unwin Australia Pty Ltd,
8 Napier Street, North Sydney, NSW 2060, Australia

First published in 1984
Second impression 1984
Third impression 1987

British Library Cataloguing in Publication Data

Brubaker, Rogers
   The limits of rationality.—(Controversies in sociology; 16)
1. Weber, Max   2. Sociology
I. Title   II. Series
301'.092'4   HM22.G3W4
ISBN 0-04-301172-1
ISBN 0-04-301173-X Pbk

Library of Congress Cataloging in Publication Data

Brubaker, Rogers.
   The limits of rationality.
(Controversies in sociology; 16)
Bibliography: p.
Includes index.
1. Weber, Max, 1864–1920.   2. Sociology—Germany.
3. Rationalism.   4. Rationalism—Moral and ethical
aspects.   I. Title   II. Series.
HM22.G3W42367   1984   301'.092'4   83-15152
ISBN 0-04-301172-1
ISBN 0-04-301173-X (pbk.)

Set in 10 on 12 point Times by Computape (Pickering) Ltd
and printed in Great Britain
by Billing and Sons Ltd, Worcester

61,735

Contents

Preface   *page* vi

Abbreviations   vii

Introduction   1

1 The Specific and Peculiar Rationalism of Modern
   Western Civilization   8

   Capitalism and Calculability   10
   Legal Formalism   16
   Bureaucratic Administration   20
   Asceticism and the Ethic of Vocation   22
   Unifying Themes: Knowledge, Impersonality, Control   29
   Formal and Substantive Rationality   35
   The Idea of a Rational Society   43

2 The Nature and Limits of Rational Action   49

   Rational and Non-Rational Action   50
   Wertrational and *Zweckrational* Action   51
   Subjective and Objective Rationality   53
   The Limits of Objective Rationality   55

3 The Ethical Irrationality of the World   61

   The Clash of Value-Orientations   62
   The Clash of Value Spheres   69
   Value Conflict and Weber's Diagnosis
      of Modernity   82

4 Weber's Moral Vision   91

   The Ethic of Personality: from Philosophical
      Anthropology to Moral Philosophy   91
   The Limits of Moral Rationality   98
   Moral Choice in the Modern World   101
   Weber's Moral Temperament   109

Bibliography   115

Index   118

Preface

This essay explores the rich and ambiguous interplay between Max Weber's empirical work and his moral vision, between his historical and sociological analysis of the 'specific and peculiar rationalism' of modern Western civilization and his deeply ambivalent moral response to that rationalism. My premise is that Weber's empirical and moral diagnosis of modern society remains a compelling one; my aim is to reconstruct this diagnosis in a coherent and systematic fashion from the tantalizingly sketchy remarks on rationality and rationalization that are scattered throughout his work.

I would like to thank Michael Donnelly, for encouraging me to explore the moral and philosophical dimensions of Weber's concern with rationalization; Bill Heffernan, for his generous and perceptive comments on several versions of this essay; and Robert K. Merton, for his unfailingly acute criticisms, both substantive and stylistic. I am especially indebted to Tom Bottomore for his patient encouragement over the past three years, as well as for a number of insightful suggestions. Jonathan Cole and Pnina Grinberg, Director and Assistant Director, respectively, of the Center for the Social Sciences at Columbia University, generously allowed me to use the Center's facilities while revising and typing the manuscript. I am deeply grateful, finally, to Louise Newman for her unstinting intellectual and moral support.

Abbreviations

The following abbreviations are used in the text to refer to Weber's writings. In a number of instances, I have modified existing translations. In such cases, I have given the German reference first, followed by the corresponding English reference. All otherwise unidentified references in Chapter 1, pp. 16–22, are to *Economy and Society*.

German Works

GAR   *Gesammelte Aufsätze zur Religionssoziologie*, Vol. 1 (Tübingen: Mohr, 1922).

GAW   *Gesammelte Aufsätze zur Wissenschaftslehre* (Tübingen: Mohr, 1922).

GPS   *Gesammelte Politische Schriften*, 2nd edn (Tübingen: Mohr, 1958).

W & G   *Wirtschaft und Gesellschaft, Studienausgabe*, based on the 4th German edn, 2 Vols, ed. Johannes Winckelmann (Köln: Kiepenheurer & Witsch, 1964).

English Translations

AI   'Author's Introduction', in *The Protestant Ethic and the Spirit of Capitalism*, trans. Talcott Parsons (New York: Scribner's, 1958), pp. 13–31.

ALW   'Anticritical last word on *The Spirit of Capitalism*', trans. Wallace M. Davis, *American Journal of Sociology*, vol. 83, no. 5 (1978), pp. 1105–31.

Categ.   'Some categories of interpretive sociology', trans. Edith E. Graber, *The Sociological Quarterly*, vol. 22, no. 2 (1981), pp. 151–80.

E & S   *Economy and Society*, ed. Guenther Roth and Claus Wittich, 2 Vols (Berkeley: University of California Press, 1978).

FMW   *From Max Weber: Essays in Sociology*, trans. and ed.

H. H. Gerth and C. Wright Mills (New York: Oxford University Press, 1946).

GEH   *General Economic History* (New Brunswick, NJ: Transaction Books, 1981).

M   *The Methodology of the Social Sciences*, trans. and ed. Edward A. Shils and Henry A. Finch (New York: Free Press, 1949).

MU   'Marginal utility theory and "the fundamental law of psychophysics"', trans. Louis Schneider, *Social Science Quarterly*, vol. 56, no. 1 (1975), pp. 21–36.

PE   *The Protestant Ethic and the Spirit of Capitalism*, trans. Talcott Parsons (New York: Scribner's, 1958).

R Ch   *The Religion of China*, trans. Hans H. Gerth (New York: Free Press, 1951).

R & K   *Roscher and Knies: The Logical Problems of Historical Economics*, trans. Guy Oakes (New York: Free Press, 1975).

S Tr   *Max Weber: Selections in Translation*, ed. W. G. Runciman, trans. E. Matthews (Cambridge: CUP, 1978).

Soc.   'Socialism', trans. D. Hÿtch, in *Max Weber: The Interpretation of Social Reality*, ed. J. E. T. Eldridge (New York: Shocken Books, 1980), pp. 191–219.

for my parents

Introduction

The idea of rationality is a great unifying theme in Max Weber's work. Weber's seemingly disparate empirical studies converge on one underlying aim: to characterize and to explain the development of the 'specific and peculiar rationalism' that distinguishes modern Western civilization from every other. His methodological investigations emphasize the universal capacity of men to act rationally and the consequent power of social science to understand as well as to explain action. His political writings are punctuated by passionate warnings about the threat posed by unchecked bureaucratic rationalization to human freedom. And his moral reflections build on an understanding of the truly human life as one guided by reason.

Rationality, then, is an *idée-maîtresse* in Weber's work, one that links his empirical and methodological investigations with his political and moral reflections. The notion of rationality, however, is far from unequivocal; Weber himself repeatedly calls attention to its multiplicity of meanings. 'If this essay makes any contribution at all', he writes in a footnote to *The Protestant Ethic and the Spirit of Capitalism*, 'may it be to bring out the complexity of the only superficially simple concept of the rational' (PE, p. 194, n. 9). And in the text of the same essay, he notes that 'rationalism is an historical concept which covers a whole world of different things' (p. 78). Consequently, as Donald Levine has remarked, 'broad statements about "rationality" *tout court* . . . are simply unsupportable' (1982, p. 1).

Yet while Weber acknowledges, even emphasizes the many-sidedness of the idea of rationality, he frequently uses the term 'rational' without qualification or explanation. This practice places great demands on the reader, who may well become confused by Weber's apparently casual and unsystematic usage. Again and again, for example, Weber characterizes various— and apparently quite heterogeneous—aspects of both ascetic Protestantism and modern capitalism as 'rational'. Thus modern capitalism is defined by the rational (deliberate and systematic) pursuit of profit through the rational (systematic and calculable) organization of formally free labor and through rational (impersonal, purely instrumental) exchange on the market, guided by rational (exact, purely quantitative) accounting procedures and guaranteed by rational (rule-governed, predictable) legal and political systems. Ascetic Protestantism is characterized by rational (methodical) self-control and by the rational (purposeful) devotion to rational (sober, scrupulous) economic action as a rational (psychologically efficacious and logically intelligible) means of relieving the intolerable pressure imposed on individuals by the rational (consistent) doctrine of predestination.

No fewer than sixteen apparent meanings of 'rational' can be culled from this highly schematic summary of Weber's characterization of modern capitalism and ascetic Protestantism: deliberate, systematic, calculable, impersonal, instrumental, exact, quantitative, rule-governed, predictable, methodical, purposeful, sober, scrupulous, efficacious, intelligible and consistent. Even allowing for some overlap among these various meanings, the reader may well be perplexed by what appears to be a baffling multiplicity of denotations and connotations.[1]

Underlying Weber's seemingly casual use of 'rational', however, is a coherent theoretical perspective, grounded in systematic comparative research. Central to this perspective is the notion of the 'specific and peculiar rationalism of Western culture' (AI, p. 26). Chapter 1 elucidates this quintessential Weberian notion by analyzing patterns of rationality and processes of rationalization in the spheres of economic life, law, administration, and religious ethics. In each of these institutional spheres, rationalization has involved the depersonalization of social relationships, the refinement of techniques of calculation, the enhancement of the social importance of specialized knowledge, and the extension of technically rational control over both natural and social processes. It is this common pattern that defines what is 'specific and peculiar' about Western rationalism.

Weber was not, of course, the first to stress the unique rationality of the modern Western social order. The progressive embodiment of reason in social institutions and practices had been a central theme of Voltaire, Montesquieu and Diderot, of Kant and Hegel, of Comte, Tönnies and Simmel.[2] Today, however, we are inclined to regard pre-Weberian discussions of the rationality of modern society as empirically oversimplified or morally overoptimistic—as implausible descriptions or naive celebrations of a 'progress' in which we no longer believe. Weber's conceptions of rationality and rationalization, on the other hand, speak directly to our experience—and our anxieties—in 'a world increasingly shaped by scientists, industrialists, and bureaucrats' (Levine, 1981a, p. 5).

If we find Weber's discussion of rationality challenging and evocative today, more than sixty years after his death, this is above all because of the marked ambivalence of his attitude toward Western rationalism. Weber breaks decisively with the 'optimistic faith [of the Enlightenment] in the theoretical and practical rationalizability of reality' (M, p. 85). In no sphere of life, according to Weber, has rationalization unambiguously advanced human well-being. The rationalization of economic production, for example, has created the 'iron cage' of capitalism, a 'tremendous cosmos' that constrains individuals from without, determining their lives 'with irresistible force' (PE, p. 181). The rational, impersonal, calculating conduct that the capitalist economic order requires of individuals, furthermore, is 'an abomination to every system of fraternal ethics' (E&S, p. 637). In the domain of administration, rationalization entails dehumanization: it requires the complete elimination 'from official business [of] love, hatred, and all purely personal, irrational, and emotional elements which escape calculation' (E&S, p. 975). And the more rational bureaucratic administration becomes, the more the individual bureaucrat is reduced to a 'small cog in a ceaselessly moving mechanism which prescribes to him an essentially fixed route of march' (E&S, p. 988). In the domain of thought, finally, the rise of modern science leads to the 'disenchantment of the world' and creates a deep tension between the basic demand that life and the world have a coherent overall meaning and the increasingly evident impossibility of determining this meaning scientifically. The extension of scientific knowledge, to be sure, enhances man's rational control over social and natural processes. But while this control has made possible dramatic improvements in material well-being, it has also made possible the development of increasingly sophisticated techniques for the 'political, social, educational, and propagandistic manipulation and domination of human beings' (M, p. 35).

Rationalization, then, far from automatically promoting human welfare, is a morally and politically problematic development. This theme is introduced in the final two sections of Chapter 1, which explore the idea that there is an irreconcilable tension between *formal* and *substantive* rationality. This notion is fundamental to Weber's social thought, linking his empirical analysis of modern society with his ambivalent moral response to it. From the point of view of the purely formal objective of maximizing the calculability of action—purely formal because maximally calculable action can be oriented to any of an infinite variety of possible substantive ends— capitalism, science, technology, and the modern legal and administrative system are highly rational. Such purely formal rationality, however, is in perpetual tension with substantive rationality, meaning rationality from the point of view of some particular substantive end, value or belief. The antagonism between the formal rationality of the modern socio-economic order and its substantive irrationality from the point of view of the values of equality, fraternity and *caritas* is 'one of the most important sources of all "social" problems, and above all, of the problems of socialism' (E&S, p. 111).

The distinction between formal and substantive rationality implies that what is rational from one point of view may be non-rational or irrational from another, and vice versa. The implications of this relational, 'perspectivist' (Kalberg, 1980, p. 1155) conception of rationality are clear—and sobering. To the extent that people share ends and beliefs, they can agree in their judgments of rationality and irrationality; but to the extent ends and beliefs diverge, so too will judgments of rationality and irrationality. According to Weber, social life is marked by perennial, indeed intensifying conflict over ends (especially ultimate ends) and beliefs (especially life-orienting metaphysical beliefs)—conflict that cannot be resolved through any neutral procedure. Consequently, Weber believes in the irreconcilability of conflicting judgments of rationality and irrationality and—a corollary of this—in the limits of rationality as an organizing principle of social life.

This notion of the limits of rationality is explored in Chapters 2, 3, and 4. In Chapter 2, I shift from the perspective of historical sociology to that of philosophical psychology, from a macroscopic focus on the broad outlines of the modern Western social order to a microscopic focus on the anatomy of rational action. For it is in the analysis of rational action—and particularly in the distinction between the *subjective* and the *objective* rationality of action—that Weber's notion of the limits of rationality appears most clearly. Subjective rationality depends on the clarity and self-consciousness of the actor's inner orientation, objective rationality on the extent to which action measures up to an objective standard. As an advocate and practitioner of interpretive (*verstehende*) sociology, committed to explaining social phenomena in terms of the subjective meaning of individual action, Weber is primarily interested in the various forms and functions of subjective rationality. But as a philosopher, committed to specifying the relation between scientific knowledge and human action, he is interested in the nature and limits of objective rationality. Judgments of objective rationality, Weber argues, are possible only from a purely technical point of view— only when the problem is to determine the most rational means to a precisely specified end. While he acknowledges the fundamental significance of objective technical rationalization in modern society, Weber stresses the idea that only a narrowly defined class of problems—those involving no conflict over ends or values—have objectively or technically rational solutions. The most pressing problems of social life do involve the clash of ends and values and thus, according to Weber, cannot be solved in an objectively rational manner.

Underlying Weber's emphasis on the limits of rationality is the idea that irreconcilable value conflict is endemic in the modern social world. This idea is analyzed in Chapter 3. Value conflict, according to Weber, occurs on two levels: on the level of individual value-orientations, and on the level of supra-individual value spheres. His discussion of value-orientations belongs to a well-defined tradition of ethical relativism and subjectivism: value-orientations are essentially subjective, and therefore conflict among them cannot be rationally resolved. His argument about value spheres, in contrast, defies easy characterization. It rests on a quasi-sociological, quasi-philosophical notion that the social world is composed of a number of distinct provinces of activity, each having its own inherent dignity and its own immanent norms. It is these autonomous realms of activity that Weber calls value spheres. On this plane, value conflict arises not from differences in the subjective value-orientations of individuals, but from objective differences in the inner structure of different forms of social action. The process of rationalization, according to Weber, intensifies this conflict by bringing ever more clearly to consciousness the autonomy and incommensurability of the various value spheres (in particular the religious, political, economic, esthetic, erotic and intellectual spheres of value).

The final chapter explores Weber's moral vision. Weber of course sees himself as an empirical scientist, not as a moral philosopher. Yet moral concerns underlie and animate all his sociological work, and in particular his investigation of the nature and limits of rationality. As Günter Abramowski (1966, p. 14) has noted,

> The driving motive behind the scientific question of the rationality of European culture is the existential question: what do rational capitalism, rational science and rational bureaucracy mean for our humanity? How are human freedom, responsible action and a meaningful way of life possible in the face of the inexorably progressing bureaucratization of life and the scientific disenchantment of the world?

In some respects, rationalization is morally disabling, hindering individuals from leading meaningful and autonomous lives. The ever-widening reach of capitalism and bureaucracy, for example, threatens to curtail individual freedom from without, while the steady diffusion of a purely instrumental (*zweckrational*) orientation erodes ultimate value commitments and thereby threatens to subvert individual autonomy from within. Yet in other respects, rationalization is morally enabling. The extension of scientific knowledge about man and nature, in particular, affords man the opportunity to achieve the special kind of moral dignity that Weber associates with the ethic of responsibility. At the heart of Weber's moral reflections, in short, is a deeply ambivalent attitude toward the processes of rationalization that have shaped and that continue to shape the modern social world.

Weber's ideas about rationality are central to his sociological work, and they are central to his moral perspective. But these ideas are neither easily accessible nor easily understandable, in part because Weber never systematized them, in part because his work is usually encountered piecemeal and seldom studied in its entirety. It is my aim to reconstruct Weber's rich but fragmented discussion of rationality, rationalism and rationalization in a systematic fashion, so as to clarify the intimate and ambiguous interplay between his sociological work and his moral outlook.

NOTES TO INTRODUCTION

1 Interesting attempts to sort out and systematize the various meanings of 'rationality' in Weber's work have been made by Eisen (1978), Kalberg (1980) and Levine (1981a, 1982).
2 In his excellent article 'Rationality and freedom: Weber and beyond' (1981a), Donald Levine includes a short discussion of the conceptions of rationality held by Kant, Hegel, Tönnies and Simmel.

1

The Specific and Peculiar Rationalism of Modern Western Civilization

A few months before his death in June 1920, Max Weber wrote a short introduction for his *Collected Essays in the Sociology of Religion*.[1] This 'preliminary remark', as he entitled it with deceptive modesty, contains what Benjamin Nelson (1974) has called the 'master clue' to Weber's lifelong scholarly intentions. For here Weber makes explicit the underlying universal–historical perspective that endows his vast, fragmented and apparently heterogeneous corpus of empirical studies[2] with thematic coherence. Basic to this perspective are two ideas: first, that modern Western civilization differs from all others in its 'specific and peculiar rationalism'; and second, that the central task of universal history is to characterize and explain this unique rationalism (AI, p. 26).[3]

Weber is quick to point out that 'rational', 'rationalism' and 'rationalization' are by no means unambiguous terms:

> There is, for example, rationalization of mystical contemplation ... just as much as there are rationalizations of economic life, of technique, of scientific research, of military training, of law and administration. Furthermore, each one of these fields may be rationalized from many different ultimate points of view and toward many different ultimate ends, and what is rational from one point of view may well be irrational from another. Hence rationalizations of the most varied character-have existed in various departments of life in all civilizations. (GAR, pp. 11–12; AI, p. 26)

The systematic ambiguity surrounding the notions of rationalism and rationalization makes it necessary to specify 'which spheres of social life are rationalized, and in what direction' (GAR, p. 12; AI, p. 26). Only in this way can the 'special peculiarity' of modern Western rationalism—and thus the distinctiveness of the modern Western social order—be made clear. And only in this way can one begin to fulfill what Weber identifies as the central task of social science: to understand the 'characteristic unique-ness [*Eigenart*] of the reality in which we move' (M, p. 72).

The 'reality in which we move', for Weber as for Marx, is dominated by capitalism, 'the most fateful force in our modern life' (AI, p. 17). And the most salient characteristic of modern industrial capitalism, according to Weber, is its thoroughgoing rational calculability. This chapter begins, then, with an analysis of the rationality of the capitalist economy. Next I discuss law and bureaucratic administration, characterized by Weber as rational because of their impersonal objectivity and their reliance on formalized rules and procedures. Common to the rationality of industrial capitalism, formalistic law and bureaucratic administration is its objectified, institutionalized, supra-individual form: in each sphere, rationality is embodied in the social structure and confronts individuals as something exter-nal to them. The development of rationality in this objectified form, according to Weber, presupposed the prior development within individuals of a certain highly peculiar kind of rational inner orientation (AI, pp. 26–7). This process of internal or subjective rationalization is discussed in Section 4, which focuses on the development among ascetic Protestants of a rigorously disciplined way of life (*Lebensführung*) based on constant self-scrutiny and methodical self-control.

Despite their historical interconnections, processes of rationalization in the spheres of economic life, law, adminis-tration, and religious ethics cannot be collapsed into a single overarching development. Rationalization, for Weber, is not a single process but a multiplicity of distinct though interrelated processes arising from different historical sources, proceeding at different rates, and furthering different interests and values. Still, these various processes of rationalization have notable structural similarities. I try to capture these common structural components in Section 5 by tracing three motifs—those of increasing knowledge, growing impersonality and enhanced control—that recur in all Weber's discussions of the rationality of the modern social order. The chapter's concluding sections examine another unifying theme: the idea that the rationality of modern capitalism, law, bureaucracy and vocational asceticism is purely formal, and that this rationality may be judged highly *irrational* from a substantive or evaluative point of view. Above all, it is this purely formal character, this indifference to all substantive ends and values, that defines what is unique—as well as what is morally and politically problematic—about Western rationalism.

CAPITALISM AND CALCULABILITY

The essence of modern capitalism, according to Weber, is its rationality.[4] To begin with, exchange in the market, the basis of the capitalist economic order, is 'the archetype of all rational social action'. Unhampered by sacred taboos, by traditional status-group privileges, or by any 'obligations of brotherliness or reverence', market transactions are determined solely by the 'purposeful pursuit of interests', by an 'orientation to the commodity and only to that' (E&S, pp. 635–6). They are rational in the negative sense of being free from the constraints of tradition and sentiment and in the positive sense of being purely instrumental (*zweckrational*), determined by an orientation to the set of opportunities for exchange and to these alone (E&S, pp. 82, 84). The market is the paradigm of rationality in this double sense, for market exchange, more than any other type of activity, is determined by the deliberate and calculating pursuit of self-interest and is free from the multifarious fetters of tradition and the capricious influence of feelings.[5]

Here, as throughout his empirical work, Weber uses 'rational' in a non-evaluative sense. His characterization of market relationships as rational implies no moral approval of these relationships; he explicitly notes that the very rationality and impersonality of pure market relationships is 'an abomination to every system of fraternal ethics' (E&S, p. 637). Like 'legitimacy' in Weber's sociology of domination and 'validity' in his sociology of law, 'rationality' is a neutral analytical concept, purged of the normative meaning it has in other contexts. This is not to deny that Weber harbors strong—though ambivalent—attitudes toward those aspects of the modern social order that he characterizes as rational. These attitudes, however, do not inhere in the term 'rational', which remains evaluatively neutral, conveying neither approbation nor condemnation.

Market exchange, then, is rational to the extent that it involves the calculating, purely instrumental orientation of economic action to opportunities for exchange and to these alone. But this is only one aspect of the rationality of modern capitalism. Just as important is the use of money accounting as a means of economic calculation and decision-making. While the social structure of market exchange elicits the *subjective disposition* to act on the basis of impersonal calculations, money accounting provides an *objectified, supra-individual technology* for carrying out these calculations, for determining unambiguously the 'best', meaning most profitable, opportunity for exchange.[6]

Monetary calculation is inherently quantitative: every good and service, every asset and liability, every factor that is (literally) 'taken into account' is assigned a numerical money value. Quantitative calculation, for Weber, is a rational means of orienting economic activity because it is exact and unambiguous:

> From a purely technical point of view, money is the most 'perfect' means of economic calculation. That is, it is formally the most rational means of orienting economic activity. Calculation in terms of money is thus the specific means of rational economic provision. (E&S, p. 86)

Monetary calculation, like market exchange, is rational only in a purely formal, non-evaluative sense. Weber explicitly contrasts the *formal* rationality of money accounting with what he calls the *substantive* rationality of economic action, the latter an inherently evaluative concept denoting the degree to which an economic system provides for the needs, furthers the ends, or accords with the values of a given social group. Moreover, he stresses the irreconcilable tension between extreme formal rationality, which requires treating the individual worker purely as a means, as a calculable instrument of production just like any material means of production, and substantive rationality. (See pp. 35–43 for a more extensive discussion of the tension between formal and substantive rationality).

The modern economy, then, is characterized by a double rationality: subjectively rational (purely instrumental) market transactions are guided by objectively rational (purely quantitative) calculations. Yet market exchange and monetary calculation alone do not define modern capitalism. For while they have developed to an unprecedented degree under modern capitalist conditions, they existed for thousands of years all over the world before the development of modern capitalism. Modern industrial capitalism is based not simply on monetary calculation but on a technically perfected form of capital accounting, not simply on market exchange but on the continuous market struggle of profit-making, bureaucratically organized enterprises employing formally free labor. These specific characteristics of modern capitalism converge on the idea of calculability—not, however, the calculability inherent in the use of money, but a much more thoroughgoing calculability based on the technique of capital accounting, on rigorous factory discipline and the precise control by owners of all human and non-human means of production, on a predictable legal and administrative system, and on the 'extension of productivity of labor ... through the subordination of the process of production to scientific points of view' (PE, p. 75).

Weber's emphasis on calculability as the essential characteristic of modern capitalism involves two distinct strands of analysis. First, the production process itself—the performance of the human and non-human means of production—is calculable. Secondly, the legal and administrative environment is calculable: the actions of judges and bureaucrats, in so far as they affect economic conduct, can be reliably predicted.

The calculability of the production process rests on specific institutional foundations. Salient among these is the entrepreneur's legally assured control over workplace, tools, machinery, sources of power, and raw materials—what Weber calls 'the complete appropriation of all material means of production by owners' (E&S, p. 161). Exact calculability depends on this centralization of control: the entrepreneur can be sure of the performance of factors of production only in so far as he controls them. Monopolization of control by entrepreneurs presupposes the 'expropriation of the individual worker from ownership of the means of production' (E&S, p. 137). Weber of course follows Marx here. But for Weber, the expropriation of the individual from the material means of his activity and livelihood is not a phenomenon peculiar to the capitalist firm. It is just as characteristic of the modern state, army, church, and university (E&S, pp. 223, 980–3; Soc., pp. 197–9). This fundamental fact of the ' "separation" of the worker from the material means of production, destruction, administration, academic research, and finance' (E&S, p. 1394)—conditioned partly by the nature of modern technology, which is typically too large, expensive or sophisticated to be controlled by the individual worker, and partly by the greater efficiency of centrally organized activity—is the cornerstone of Weber's theory of bureaucracy (see pp. 20–2 below). Thus the rationalization of economic activity, in so far as it depends on the centralization of control over the material means of production, is part of a much broader process of rationalization that Weber subsumes under the notion of bureaucratization.

Technical knowledge is the second factor on which the calculability of the production process depends. Effective control over the means of production, as distinguished from the mere power to dispose of them at will, itself depends on reliable technical knowledge. Highly refined technical knowledge, in turn, depends ultimately on 'the peculiar features of Western science, especially the mathematically and experimentally exact natural sciences with their precise rational foundations' (S Tr, p. 338; cf. AI, p. 24). (The 'practical and ... methodical inclusion of natural science in the service of the economy', according to Weber, is important not only as a source of the exact calculability of the production process but also as 'one of the keystones in the development of the regulation of life in general' (ALW, p. 1129). Weber nowhere systematically expounds his views on the relation between the development of modern science and processes of rationalization in other domains, but it is clear that he regards the theoretical development and practical application of natural science as a central component of the distinctively Western course of rationalization, as much because of its general effect in fostering a 'rationalist and antitraditionalist spirit' (ALW, pp. 1128–9) as because of its specific contributions to technical progress.)

Finally, the calculability of the production process depends on the uniquely Western system of formally free labor and on the disciplined control of workers by entrepreneurs. Maximum calculability, according to Weber, is achieved not with slave labor, but with labor that is formally free yet economically compelled—under the 'whip of hunger' (GEH, p. 277)—to sell its services on the market:

> When workers are employed for wages, the following advantages to industrial profitability and efficiency are conspicuous [Weber is comparing formally free labor with slave labor]: (a) capital risk and the necessary capital investment are smaller; (b) the costs of reproduction and of bringing up children fall entirely on the worker. His wife and children must seek employment on their own account; (c) largely for this reason, the risk of dismissal is an important incentive to the maximization of production; (d) it is possible to select the labor force according to ability and willingness to work. (E&S, p. 163; cf. pp. 113, 129, 150–1)

Labor must be subject to strict—and strictly rational—discipline. Weber cites the Taylor system of 'scientific management' as the limiting case of discipline and control based on knowledge:

> Discipline in the factory has a completely rational basis. With the help of suitable methods of measurement, the optimum profitability of the individual worker is calculated like that of any material means of production. On this basis, the American system of 'scientific management' triumphantly proceeds with its rational conditioning and training of work performances, thus drawing the ultimate conclusions from the mechanization and discipline of the plant. The psychophysical apparatus of man is completely adjusted to the demands of the outer world, the tools, the machines—in short, it is functionalized, and the individual is shorn of his natural rhythm as determined by his organism; in line with the demands of work procedure, he is attuned to a new rhythm through the functional specialization of muscles and through

the creation of an optimal economy of physical effort. (E&S, p. 1156)

The fact that maximum calculability in economic (and other) organizations requires the disciplined control of some human beings by others is another instance of the antagonism—endemic in the modern social order—between formal and substantive rationality.

Industrial capitalism is characterized not only by the exact calculability of the production process, but also by the calculability of the legal and administrative environment within which economic action takes place. Modern capitalism, Weber argues, presupposes this calculability:

> The modern capitalist enterprise ... presupposes a legal and administrative system whose functioning can be rationally predicted, at least in principle, by virtue of its fixed general norms, just like the expected performance of a machine. (E&S, p. 1394; cf. pp. 1094–5)

Industrial capitalism could not have developed in the context of a legal system in which decisions were made on the basis of a judge's sense of equity in a given case (E&S, pp. 976–8), on the basis of revelation (by oracle or ordeal), or on the basis of strict adherence to sacred tradition. Nor could modern capitalism have developed in the context of a patrimonial political system in which administrative decisions were carried out in accordance with the inflexible requirements of tradition or the arbitrary discretion of the ruler. Earlier forms of capitalism, particularly those Weber groups under the heading 'politically oriented capitalism' (E&S, pp. 164–6), could and did flourish in such unpredictable legal and administrative environments. But modern capitalist firms, run on the basis of an accounting technique requiring precise calculation, are 'much too vulnerable to irrationalities of law and administration' (E&S, p. 1395) to develop or survive outside a predictable legal and administrative environment. Thus the rationalization of law and administration, according to Weber, is a prerequisite for the rationalization of economic life.

Quite apart from its significance as a precondition of capitalist development, the rationality of the modern legal and administrative order deserves discussion in its own right. For if capitalism is one of the two main empirical referents of Weber's conception of the 'specific and peculiar rationalism of Western culture', rational law and bureaucratic administration together comprise the other.

LEGAL FORMALISM

Modern capitalist rationality is rooted in calculability; modern legal rationality in formalism.[7] Like many of Weber's most fruitful notions—bureaucracy, charisma and the spirit of capitalism come immediately to mind—legal formalism is not a concept with a single unambiguous meaning but a complex, multifaceted conceptual construct that resists encapsulation in a definition. One aspect of legal formalism can best be grasped by contrasting the highly articulated and differentiated structure of the modern Western legal order with the undifferentiated structure of the Asiatic legal order. In Asia

> religious prescriptions were never differentiated from secular rules, and . . . the characteristically theocratic combination of religious and ritualistic prescriptions with legal rules remained unchanged. In this case, there arose a featureless conglomeration of ethical and legal duties, moral exhortations and legal commandments without formalized explicitness, and the result was a specifically *non-formal* type of law. (E&S, p. 810; all references in this and the next section, unless otherwise identified, are to *Economy and Society*.)

In the West, by contrast, a differentiated legal order emerged gradually and unevenly out of an originally undifferentiated amalgam of legal, religious, ethical and conventional regulations. The modern legal order is based on a series of explicitly formulated distinctions. One of these is the distinction between substantive and procedural law—between 'rules of law to be applied in the process of law-finding [legal decision-making] and rules regarding that process itself' (p. 654). A second is the distinction between questions of law and questions of fact, the latter to be ascertained through a specialized rational procedure involving written documents and the examination of witnesses (pp. 811, 817, 830). Third, and most important here, is the distinction between law-making and law-finding: between the establishment of general legal rules and the application of those rules in particular cases.

Modern law-making, in the form of the deliberate enactment of legislation, is rational in a double sense. First, legislation consists in the self-conscious, deliberate enactment of new legal norms. Weber contrasts this both with the unconscious emergence of new legal norms through 'unperceived changes in meaning' (pp. 754–5) and with the idea, prevalent in traditional societies, that legal norms cannot be created through conscious enactment (pp. 227, 760). Secondly, the procedure whereby new legal norms are created is itself governed by legal norms: legislation is enacted 'in conformity with the formal constitutional requirements' (p. 753). Such rule-governed legislative procedure is rational in contrast to the arbitrary imposition of new legal norms through charismatic revelation (p. 761).

Modern law-finding, as distinguished from law-making, involves the application of general legal norms to the concrete facts of a particular case. In the ideally rational case, legal decisions made in this manner can be reliably predicted by interested parties:

> judicial formalism enables the legal system to operate like a technically rational machine. Thus it guarantees to individuals and groups within the system a relative maximum of freedom, and greatly increases for them the possibility of predicting the legal consequences of their actions. Procedure becomes a specified type of pacified contest, bound to fixed and inviolable 'rules of the game'. (p. 811)

Weber contrasts the rational predictability of modern law-finding with two kinds of informal, unpredictable, and in this sense irrational adjudication: first, adjudication based on oracles, ordeals or other 'means which cannot be controlled by the intellect' (p. 656); and second, 'kadi-justice', in which legal decisions derive not from the application of general rules to a particular body of facts but from the judge's 'sense of equity in a given case' (pp. 1115, 1395). Wherever such incalculable modes of law-finding prevail, Weber argues, they will impede economic rationalization. Rationalization in the legal sphere is thus bound up with rationalization in the economic sphere.

The formalism of the modern Western legal system refers not only to the mode of establishing legal norms and to the mode of applying them in particular cases but also to the nature of the legal norms themselves. Legal norms are formal to the extent that they are general principles, as opposed to particular 'reasons relevant in the decision of concrete individual cases' (p. 655), and to the extent that these general principles are not of a 'substantive' character, in Weber's special sense of the word. As distinguished from substantive rules, purely formal legal rules take into account only 'unambiguous general characteristics of the facts' (pp. 656–7) and thus avoid reference to substantive ethical or political ends, at least in so far as these cannot be construed unambiguously. Pure formalism, Weber grants, is an ideal-typical limiting case, not an accurate description of the modern legal order; in fact, many modern laws instruct the judge to 'render his decision on the basis of ethics, equity, or expediency' (p. 645; cf. pp. 882–9, 979)—i.e. on the basis of substantive as opposed to purely formal considerations. Nonetheless, the modern Western legal order is characterized not only by formal modes of establishing legal norms and applying them in particular cases but also, to a greater extent than any other legal order, by a body of abstract, general legal norms involving no reference to substantive ends or values. These norms, in the ideally rational case, are systematically related to one another, so as to constitute a 'logically clear, internally consistent, and, at least in theory, gapless system of rules under which ... all conceivable fact situations must be capable of being logically subsumed' (p. 656).

Extensive freedom of contract, closely related to the expansion of the market, is another aspect of the modern fomalistic legal order. Just as the market mechanism permits—indeed, forces—the individual to secure his economic existence through formally free market transactions, so freedom of contract permits the individual to regulate his economic relations through formally autonomous legal transactions. 'The increased importance of the private law contract', Weber writes, 'is thus the legal reflex of the market orientation of our society' (p. 672). Weber distinguishes the traditional 'status contract' from the modern 'instrumental contract' (*Zweck-Kontrakt*). The status contract effected a change in the

> total legal situation ... and the social status of the persons involved ... By means of such a contract a person was to become somebody's child, father, wife, brother, master, slave, kin, comrade-in-arms, protector, client, follower, vassal, subject [or] friend ... [This did not] mean that a certain performance ... contributing to the attainment of some specific object, was reciprocally guaranteed or expected ... The contract rather meant that the person would 'become' something different in quality (or status) from the quality he possessed before. (p. 672)

Instrumental contracts, in contrast, involve no change in status; they aim 'at some specific (especially economic) performance or result' (p. 673). This is true above all of the money contract, the 'archetypal instrumental contract': a 'specific, quantitatively delimited, qualityless, abstract ... agreement' (W&G, p. 515; E&S, p. 674). The pure formalism of the money contract corresponds to the formalism of abstract enacted norms. And its purely instrumental and impersonal character mirrors the instrumental, impersonal nature of market transactions.

Formal legal equality prevails in the domain of enacted law and in the domain of contractual agreement. Enacted norms apply equally to all, 'without respect of person' (E&S, p. 699), and all have the freedom to 'set the content of contracts in accordance with [their] desires' (p. 729). Of course formal freedom of contract does not guarantee that everyone will be equally able to stipulate the terms of contractual agreements, for legally protected inequalities in the distribution of property generate inequalities in bargaining power. Freedom of contract enables an economically powerful employer, for example, to 'impose his terms' upon the worker, who is constrained to accept them by his 'more pressing economic need' (p. 730).

Legal formalism, like economic calculability, is rational only in a purely formal sense. To be sure, formal justice guarantees the 'maximum freedom for the interested parties to represent their formal legal interests'. But on account of the 'unequal distribution of economic power, which the system of formal justice legalizes, this very freedom must time and again produce consequences which are contrary to the substantive postulates of religious ethics or of political expediency' (p. 812). There is thus an 'insoluble conflict between the formal and the substantive principles of justice' (p. 893), just as there is an irreconcilable tension between formal and substantive rationality in the economic sphere. (The antagonism between the purely formal rationality of the modern economic and legal order and its substantive irrationality from the standpoint of certain deeply rooted value commitments—a fundamental theme in Weber's social thought—is examined in pp. 35–43 of this chapter.)

BUREAUCRATIC ADMINISTRATION

Modern administration, Weber argues, is increasingly—and inevitably—bureaucratic. This is true not only in the sphere of the state, but in all domains of social life. Churches, armies, political parties, economic enterprises, interest groups, associations of all kinds, endowments, universities—all are subject to the inexorable advance of bureaucratization. 'It would be sheer illusion', Weber writes, 'to think for a moment that continuous administrative work can be carried out in any field except by means of [bureaucratic] officials . . . The whole pattern of everyday life is cut to fit this framework' (E&S, p. 223).

The indispensability of bureaucratic administration is grounded in its thoroughgoing rationality.[8] One aspect of this rationality is its formalism. Like the modern legal order, bureaucratic administration has a formally articulated and differentiated structure. Formal rules delimit the 'jurisdictional area' of each agency, specify the distribution of authority within the agency, spell out the duties associated with each position, and establish a regular procedure for carrying out these duties (pp. 218, 956–7). Formal, abstract, general rules, moreover, are the specific means of bureaucratic administration:

the authority to order certain matters by decree—which has been legally granted to an agency—does not entitle the agency to regulate the matter by individual commands given for each case, but only to regulate the matter abstractly. This stands in extreme contrast to the regulation of all relationships through individual privileges and bestowals of favor, which . . . is absolutely dominant in patrimonialism. (p. 958)

The formalism of bureaucratic administration is expressed, finally, in a distinctive ethos. Devoted to 'impersonal and functional purposes', the bureaucratic official acts in a 'spirit of formalistic impersonality . . . without hatred or passion, and hence without affection or enthusiasm' (pp. 225, 959). The formalistic impersonality of the bureaucratic ethos corresponds to the pure instrumentalism and impersonality of market transactions and money contracts, and the execution of official business 'without regard for persons' corresponds to the formal equality of all persons in the modern legal order.

A second aspect of the rationality of bureaucracy is its technical efficiency, which Weber characterizes in mechanistic terms:

> The fully developed bureaucratic apparatus compares with other organizations exactly as does the machine with the non-mechanical modes of production. Precision, speed, unambiguity . . . continuity . . . unity, strict subordination, reduction of friction and of material and personal costs—these are raised to the optimum point in the strictly bureaucratic administration. (p. 973)

The quasi-mechanical efficiency of bureaucratic administration 'makes possible a particularly high degree of calculability of results' (p. 223).[9] This calculability benefits capitalist entrepreneurs, who 'must be able to count on the . . . rational, predictable functioning of . . . administrative agencies' (p. 1095). More ominously, it also makes the bureaucratic apparatus a 'highly developed power instrument in the hands of its controller' (p. 991; cf. p. 987).

Bureaucratic administration is rational not only because of its impersonal formalism and its machine-like efficiency but also— and most fundamentally—because it is based on knowledge. More precisely, it is based on specialized technical expertise, which becomes increasingly indispensable to administration as the technical and economic base of modern life becomes ever more complex. By placing a premium on technical expertise, bureaucratization contributes in a very general way to the rationalization of life: it 'furthers the development of rational "matter-of-factness" [*Sachlichkeit*] and the personality type of the professional expert' (p. 998), and it tends to substitute certification by education for certification by ancestry as a means of monopolizing 'socially and economically advantageous positions' (p. 1000).

Like industrial capitalism and formalistic law, bureaucratic administration is rational only in a purely formal, non-evaluative sense. And the greater its formal rationality, the more vulnerable it becomes to criticism for its substantive irrationality. Thus what is 'appraised as its special virtue by capitalism'—the spirit of formalistic impersonality—may be condemned from another perspective as dehumanizing:

> Bureaucracy develops the more perfectly, the more it is 'dehumanized', the more completely it succeeds in eliminating from official business love, hatred, and all purely personal . . . and emotional elements which escape calculation. (p. 975)

Similarly, the more closely a bureaucratic organization approximates a technically efficient machine, the greater the danger to individual freedom and dignity: the individual official is reduced to a 'small cog in a ceaselessly moving mechanism which prescribes to him an essentially fixed route of march' (p. 988). Bureaucracy, moreover, induces an ethic of adjustment (*Anpassung*), of 'adaptation to the possible' (M, p. 24), an ethic that discourages the value-oriented striving that Weber sees as central to the development of autonomous moral personality (see Chapter 4). Finally, the more important the role played by technical expertise in the functioning of a bureaucratic organization, the less responsive the organization will be to the control of those who lack such expertise: bureaucracy, in short, invites technocracy.

ASCETICISM AND THE ETHIC OF VOCATION

Weber analyzes the modern social order not only from a static but also from a dynamic perspective: he aims not only to delineate the 'special peculiarity' of contemporary Western rationalism but also to elucidate its historical development (AI, p. 26). In other words, he is concerned as much with the process of rationalization as with the product, rationality. This process, Weber argues, is *not* a gradual and continuous one. The 'roads to modernity', in Benjamin Nelson's apt formulation, are 'paved with "charismatic" breakthroughs of traditional structures' (1973, p. 78). Today, the importance of these breakthroughs is easily overlooked, for the scientific, technical, economic and administrative rationalization of life has become a self-perpetuating process, capable of inducing in individuals the subjective attitudes and dispositions needed to reproduce and reinforce the objectified, supra-individual forms of rationality embodied in the social structure. Weber makes this point explicitly with respect to capitalism:

> The capitalistic economy of the present day is an immense cosmos into which the individual is born, and which presents itself to him . . . as an unalterable order of things in which he must live. It forces the individual, in so far as he is involved in the system of market relationships, to conform to capitalistic rules of action. The manufacturer who in the long run acts counter to these norms, will just as inevitably be eliminated from the economic scene as the worker who cannot or will not adapt himself to them will be thrown into the streets without a job.
>
> Thus the capitalism of today, which has come to dominate economic life, educates and selects the economic subjects which it needs through a process of economic survival of the fittest. (PE, pp. 54–5; cf. p. 72)

Before the advent of modern capitalism, however, economic rationalization was not a self-sustaining process. Modern capitalism, according to Weber, did not develop and could not have developed directly and 'naturally' through a gradual process of rationalization from earlier forms of capitalism. The calculative rationality so firmly entrenched in the modern economic and political order is not the product of a slow and steady extension in the scope of calculating, self-interested action. Instead, the development of modern rational capitalism required a radical breakthrough in the domain of attitudes and dispositions—a breakthrough that Weber attributes to the religious ideas of the Reformation. The logical and psychological pressures generated by the ideas of Luther and Calvin led to the development of what Weber calls 'worldly asceticism'—at once a new ethical attitude and a new personality structure. This inner rationalization of the personality in the direction of unrelenting work and methodical self-control, Weber argues, provided a decisive impetus to the development of modern industrial capitalism.[10]

In *The Protestant Ethic and the Spirit of Capitalism*, Weber traces the development of worldly asceticism to four elements of Reformation doctrine. First, Luther's conception of the calling granted full moral and religious dignity to 'worldly' activity— meaning activity in ordinary social and economic settings, as opposed to activity carried out in special social settings (such as monasteries) that are organized in explicit opposition to the 'world'. The holiest task was no longer 'to surpass all worldly morality' through a monastic or other retreat from the world, but to demonstrate one's faith through worldly activity (PE, p. 121). Secondly, the Calvinist conception of an absolutely transcendental deity made true mystical union with God inconceivable: since the believer could not aspire to be the *vessel* of God, he had to think of himself as an active '*tool* of the divine will', as an instrument serving to 'increase the glory of God' through intense, single-minded, rational worldly activity (PE, pp. 113–14, emphasis added; E&S, p. 546). Thirdly, the Calvinist doctrine of the 'corruption of everything pertaining to the flesh' and Calvinism's general abhorrence of 'all the sensuous and emotional elements in culture and in religion' put a premium on strictly impersonal, radically individualistic, and thoroughly anti-hedonistic activity (PE, pp. 105–6, 109, 224 n. 30).

The central Calvinist doctrine of predestination, finally, had decisive psychological consequences. Salvation was regarded by Calvinism as an inexplicable gift of grace from an inscrutable, absolutely transcendental God (E&S, p. 572). In theory, the individual was powerless to affect his salvation and equally powerless to know his predetermined fate. Fatalism was thus 'the only *logical* consequence of predestination'. But the '*psychological* result was exactly the opposite' (PE, p. 232 n. 66, emphasis added). Individuals had a religious interest 'of absolutely dominant importance' (PE, p. 110) in ascertaining their state of grace.[11] Hence it was psychologically necessary that there be some means of determining one's eternal fate. In response to this overwhelming psychological pressure, Puritan pastors came to recommend intense, methodically controlled activity in a worldly calling as a means of 'attain[ing] certainty of one's own election' (PE, p. 111), and they came to interpret worldly economic success as a sign of God's blessing, thus relieving the intolerable psychological uncertainty imposed by the doctrine of predestination. Worldly asceticism—the disposition to work intensely and methodically in a worldly calling—is thus presented by Weber as the practical–psychological consequence of the theoretical doctrines of the Reformation, and more particularly of Calvinism.

Weber stresses the hard, relentless rationality of worldly asceticism. (Again, he uses 'rational' in a value-neutral manner and repeatedly notes the *irrationality* of worldly asceticism, considered from the point of view of personal happiness.[12]) In the first place, the rigorous self-control of the worldly ascetic is rational in the sense of anti-emotional. Thus Weber remarks on the Puritans' 'rational suppression of the mystical, in fact the whole emotional side of religion' (PE, p. 123). Moreover, *methodical* self-control is rational because it is continuous and systematic rather than occasional and haphazard: 'the moral conduct of the average man was thus deprived of its planless and unsystematic character and subjected to a consistent method for conduct as a whole' (PE, p. 117). Finally, the regulation of conduct through *conscious self-scrutiny* is rational in that it requires a 'life guided by constant thought', by 'reflection and knowledge of the self' (PE, pp. 118, 235 n. 75).[13]

Rational asceticism as such has no definite consequences—for these consequences vary with the *direction* of ascetic activity. Catholic monastic asceticism, for example, produced tremendous economic achievements, but remained 'world-rejecting' and as a result did not dramatically impinge on the economic life of society at large (PE, pp. 118–21). Puritan worldly asceticism, on the other hand, channeled concentrated and disciplined energy into economic activity in the 'world' and as a result 'did its part [albeit unintentionally] in building the tremendous cosmos of the modern economic order' (PE, p. 181). To begin with, the premium placed on continuous work in a calling and the acceptance of the accumulation of wealth as a sign that one's work had found 'favor in the sight of God' (PE, p. 162), together with the condemnation of the idle enjoyment of wealth (PE, p. 157), promoted the 'accumulation of capital through ascetic compulsion to save' (PE, p. 172). But the major significance of Puritanism for economic development, according to Weber, lies less in its encouragement of capital accumulation than in its more general contribution to the formation of a 'specifically bourgeois economic ethic' (PE, p. 176)—to what Weber calls the 'spirit of capitalism'—and thereby to the 'ascetic rationalization of the whole of economic life' (PE, p. 278 n. 85). The worldly asceticism of the Puritans was not identical with the spirit of capitalism epitomized in the writings of Ben Franklin: the former was oriented 'solely toward a transcendental end, salvation' (PE, p. 118), the latter toward the earning of money as an end in itself (PE, pp. 51–2). But the psychological pressure on the Puritan to confirm his state of grace and the interpretation of economic success as the most important sign of grace meant that worldly asceticism and the spirit of capitalism channeled conduct in the same direction. Moreover, as its primary concern with salvation ebbed, a secularized worldly asceticism became indistinguishable from the spirit of capitalism. 'The essential elements of . . . the spirit of capitalism', Weber writes, 'are the same as . . . the content of the Puritan worldly asceticism, only without the religious basis, which by Franklin's time had died away' (PE, p. 180).

The development of modern industrial capitalism, according to Weber, presupposed on the one hand an 'external' rationalization of the environment, through which technological, legal and administrative factors affecting production and exchange became increasingly calculable and thus predictable. A cluster of relatively independent historical processes—including especially the development of modern science and the emergence of the modern state with its formalistic legal system and bureaucratic administrative structure—comprised this external rationalization. But *in addition*, the development of modern capitalism presupposed an inner reorganization and rationalization of the personality. Nascent capitalist enterprises—capitalist, that is, in external form of organization—could not by themselves transform traditionalistic attitudes toward work; and modern industrial capitalism, based on the 'pursuit of profit, and forever *renewed* profit, by means of continuous, rational ... enterprise' (AI, p. 17), could not develop without such a transformation of attitudes. Before the system of industrial capitalism was firmly established, proto-capitalistic enterprises were run in a thoroughly traditionalistic manner (PE, pp. 64-7). Traditionalistic attitudes toward work—the greatest 'inner obstacle' to the development of modern capitalism—were decisively overcome only through the inner reorientation of ethical attitudes that was accomplished by ascetic Protestantism. Only when the yoke of tradition had been thrown off through this unprecedented inner rationalization of the personality did sober, scrupulous devotion to the accumulation of wealth—an attitude previously considered 'ethically unjustifiable, or at best to be tolerated'—come to be considered the 'essence of moral conduct, even commanded in the name of duty' (PE, p. 75). In sum, rationalization in the spheres of science, technology, law and administration created a calculable external environment, while an independent rationalization in the sphere of religion and ethics created a disciplined, work-centered inner orientation that turned out, by a great irony of history, to be superbly 'adapted to the peculiarities of capitalism' (PE, p. 55).[14] Both external and internal rationalizations were indispensable preconditions for the development of modern industrial capitalism.

Besides serving as a decisive stimulus 'from within' for the development of capitalism, the ascetic personality structure bequeathed to modern society by Puritanism formed the basis of what Weber calls '*Berufsmenschentum*'—the 'vocationalist' or 'professionalist' inner orientation that characterizes modern political, legal and administrative as well as economic activity. *The Protestant Ethic* thus has implications beyond the 'spirit of capitalism': in Weber's own sweeping characterization, the essay is about 'Protestant asceticism as the foundation of modern vocational civilization' (FMW, pp. 18–19).

Modern civilization is characterized by what Weber calls the '*Versachlichung der Gewaltherrschaft*' (W&G, p. 464): by the 'objectification' or 'depersonalization' of the structure of power and authority. In premodern times,

> power relationships in both the economic and political spheres have a purely personal character. In these spheres ... a whole organized structure of personal relations of subordination exists which is dominated by caprice and grace, indignation and love, and most of all by the mutual piety and devotion of masters and subalterns, after the fashion of the family. Thus, these relationships of domination have a character to which one may apply ethical requirements in the same way that one applies them to every other purely personal relationship. (E&S, p. 600; cf. pp. 584–5)

But in the modern economy and state, relationships of authority 'no longer possess this personalistic character' (E&S, p. 600). As a result, activity in these spheres cannot be meaningfully guided by ethical ideals such as *caritas* or brotherliness:

> In the economic realm the rise of capitalism makes these ideals just as meaningless as the implicit pacifist ideals of early Christianity have always been in the political realm in which all domination ultimately rests on force. (W&G, p. 902; E&S, p. 1188)

An ascetic ethic of vocation (*Berufsethik*), however, by virtue of its impersonality and objectivity, is ideally suited to action in the modern economy and in the modern state:

> Today ... the *homo politicus*, as well as the *homo oeconomicus*, performs his duty best when he acts without regard to the person in question ... without hatred and without love, without personal predilection and therefore without grace, but sheerly in accordance with the impersonal duty imposed by his calling [*sachliche Berufspflicht*]. (E&S, p. 600)

Only the impersonal ethic of vocation of worldly asceticism, Weber concludes, is an 'adequate' (*innerlich adäquat*) guide for action in a world in which economic and political relationships have been so thoroughly depersonalized and objectified (W&G, p. 464; E&S, p. 601).

Weber's summary of the unintended cultural and economic consequences of the worldly asceticism of the Puritans may serve as a conclusion:

> The curtailment of all feudal ostentation and of all irrational consumption facilitates capital accumulation ... while worldly asceticism as a whole favors the breeding and exaltation of the vocationalism [*Berufsmenschentum*] needed by capitalism and bureaucracy. Life is focused not on persons but on impersonal [*sachlich*] rational goals ... And since the success of work is the surest symptom that it pleases God, capitalist profit is one of the most important criteria for establishing that God's blessing rests on the enterprise. It is clear that this style of life is very closely related to the self-justification that is customary for bourgeois acquisition: profit and property appear not as ends in themselves but as indications of personal ability. Here has been attained the union of religious postulate and bourgeois style of life favorable to capitalism. Of course, this was not the purpose of the Puritan ethic, especially not the encouragement of money making; on the contrary ... wealth was regarded as dangerous and full of temptation. However, just as the monasteries time and again brought this temptation on themselves by virtue of the ascetic rational work and conduct of their members, so now did the pious bourgeois who lived and worked ascetically. (W&G, p. 913; E&S, p. 1200)

The worldly asceticism of the Puritans, then, contributed to the development of a distinctive *ethos*, the various aspects of which Weber describes as the 'spirit of capitalism', the 'bourgeois style of life', and the attitude toward work he calls *Berufsmenschentum*. This ethos, in turn, promoted the development of modern capitalism and bureaucracy. In this manner, the inner rationalization of the personality effected by Protestant asceticism gave a decisive impetus to the external rationalization of economic and political life and helped it develop into the self-sustaining process of rationalization that it is today.

UNIFYING THEMES: KNOWLEDGE, IMPERSONALITY, CONTROL

Weber's conception of the rationality of modern civilization, as should be evident from the preceding sections, is far from univocal. Each component of the modern Western social order surveyed above—industrial capitalism, formalistic law, bureaucratic administration, and the ascetic ethic of vocation—has its own specific mode of rationality. The multifaceted rationality of modern society, moreover, is the product of processes of rationalization occurring in several distinct spheres of social life, proceeding in various directions and arising from diverse historical sources. Yet despite this multiplicity of modes of rationality and rationalization, the 'specific and peculiar rationalism of Western culture' is not simply a conceptual mosaic, not a mere aggregation of unrelated elements. Certain thematic strands run throughout Weber's discussions of the rationality of the modern social order, cutting across the boundaries between the different spheres of social life and forming a central core of meaning. One such theme, already alluded to several times in passing, is that the rationality of modern capitalism, law, bureaucracy and vocational asceticism is purely formal, and that this very rationality may be judged highly *irrational* from a substantive or evaluative point of view. Since this distinction between formal and substantive rationality provides a key bridge between Weber's empirical analysis of modern society and his moral outlook, it calls for discussion in detail—discussion that I reserve for the next section. This section briefly traces three other thematic strands—those of knowledge, impersonality and control—that weave together the various aspects of Weber's conception of the unique rationality of modern society.

Knowledge. To act rationally, in one very general sense of this highly ambiguous expression, is to act on the basis of knowledge. Rational action in this sense is universal: all men in all societies and all epochs (though not, of course, in all of their actions) base their conduct to some extent on knowledge—especially knowledge of means–ends relations and of the probable reactions of their physical and social environment to their actions. In modern Western society, however, the rise of systematic empirical science and of scientific technology gives knowledge an importance above and beyond its universal significance as a basis for individual rational action. The growing complexity of the technical and economic base of social life, together with the inexorable advance of bureaucracy, fuels an ever-growing demand for specialized technical knowledge (*Fachwissen*). This demand determines the general character of the modern educational system, which is increasingly geared to the production of specialized technical expertise rather than to the cultivation of the overall personality. The growing demand for technical expertise also conditions the mode of stratification, for the possession of specialized technical knowledge increasingly shapes one's life chances (E&S, pp. 998–1002).

The rise of modern science is significant also as the chief agent of a more general process of intellectualization. One aspect of intellectualization is the progressive 'disenchantment of the world'—the displacement of magical and religious views of the world by the scientific view of the world as a 'causal mechanism' that, *in principle*, can be mastered by 'technical means and calculations'. The qualification is important. Intellectualization does '*not* imply an increasing general knowledge of the conditions under which one lives'. Quite the contrary: 'the "savage" knows infinitely more about the economic and social conditions of his own existence than does the "civilized man" '. None the less, intellectualization fosters the *belief* that no 'mysterious incalculable forces . . . come into play', and that one can therefore 'master all things by calculation' (*alle Dinge . . . durch Berechnen beherrschen*). It is this belief that gives a 'specifically rational flavor' to the everyday experience of modern individuals, even those with little or no scientific training (GAW, pp. 449, 536; FMW, pp. 139, 350; Categ., pp. 178–9). At the same time that it *induces* the belief that the phenomena of everyday life are calculable and therefore (in principle) controllable, disenchantment *erodes* the belief that the world has a discoverable meaning. Sharp and irreconcilable tensions arise between the deeply rooted demand that life and the world possess a coherent overall meaning and the increasingly evident impossibility of determining this meaning scientifically.

Another aspect of intellectualization is the increasing tendency for individuals to act on the basis of conscious reflection about the probable consequences of their action—a mode of orientation that Weber calls *zweckrational* (means–ends rational or instrumentally rational). *Zweckrational* action is

> determined by expectations as to the behavior of objects in the environment and of other human beings; these expectations are used as 'conditions' or 'means' for the attainment of the actor's own rationally pursued and calculated ends. (E&S, p. 24)

The displacement of 'unthinking acquiescence in customary ways' by the 'deliberate adaptation to situations in terms of self-interest' is 'one essential component of the process of "rationalization" of action' (W&G, p. 22; E&S, p. 30).

The increasing significance of knowledge in social life, in sum, is conceptualized by Weber on four levels. He stresses (1) the growing importance of specialized knowledge—or the certification that an individual possesses such knowledge—for the economy, the government, the educational system and the system of stratification; (2) the progressive displacement of the cultivated man by the specialized expert (*Fachmensch*) as an emblematic character expressing the central values of our civilization (E&S, pp. 1001–2); (3) the rational cast of everyday experience, deriving from the disenchantment and intellectualization of the world; and (4) the growing salience of individual action based on conscious reflection and calculation.

Impersonality. The modern Western social order, as noted above, is characterized by what Weber calls the '*Versachlichung der Gewaltherrschaft*'—by the 'objectification' or 'depersonalization' of the structure of power and authority in both the economic and the political realm. Market transactions are the 'most impersonal' of all social relationships (E&S, p. 636); and domination by capital (*Kapitalherrschaft*), based on the purely impersonal fact of a dominant market position, imposes on propertyless workers a 'masterless slavery' in which the behavior of the powerful and powerless alike is determined by purely objective, impersonal considerations. The impersonal laws of the marketplace are self-enforcing: disobedience 'entails economic failure and, in the long run, economic ruin' (E&S, p. 585).

Political authority, too, is subject to a 'general depersonalization' (*allgemeine Versachlichung*; W&G, p. 218; E&S, p. 294). Weber's famous typology of types of authority, the core of his political sociology, is based on a distinction between personal and impersonal forms of domination—between domination based on personal authority, whether sanctioned by sacred tradition or by individual charisma, and domination based on the impersonal authority of a system of legal rules (E&S, pp. 215–16, 954). The modern Western political order, apart from charismatic elements in the electoral process, rests almost exclusively on impersonal foundations: on legal authority, on the formal equality of all persons before the law, and on impersonal bureaucratic administration.

Impersonality, finally, is a characteristic of the specifically modern and Western vocational ethos (*Berufsethik*) and of its source, Puritan worldly asceticism. This ethos bids man fulfill his worldly tasks 'sheerly in accordance with the impersonal duty imposed by his calling [*sachliche Berufspflicht*] and not as a result of any concrete personal relationship' (E&S, p. 600). Rationalization in the direction of increasing impersonality, in sum, denotes on the one hand the objectification and depersonalization of relations of power in the political and economic spheres, and on the other hand the emergence of a new inner attitude—the Puritan-influenced ethic of vocation—appropriate to the transformed economic and political conditions.

Control. The theme of control—over material objects, over other men, over oneself—pervades Weber's discussions of rationality.[15] The scope of effective control over men and nature has widened dramatically in modern society as a result of the progress of technical rationalization in every sphere of social life—including, Weber notes explicitly, 'the political, social, educational, and propagandistic manipulation and domination of human beings' (M, p. 35). (Technical rationalization denotes the development of technically 'superior'—i.e. more efficient—means of achieving given ends, whatever the value or significance of the ends. See Chapter 2, pp. 55–8.) As scientific knowledge is embodied in ever-new practical applications, technical rationalization transforms not only economic life, with its growing dependence on scientifically grounded technology, but also military, political, artistic and even religious activity.

Above all, Weber is concerned with the extension of technically rational control over men in capitalist firms and bureaucratic administrative organizations. Such control, based on strict discipline, tends to reduce the individual to the function he performs. In the factory, for example, the 'optimum profitability of the individual worker is calculated like that of any material means of production' (E&S, p. 1156). And in 'that animated machine, the bureaucratic organization' (E&S, p. 1402), the official is only 'a small cog in a ceaselessly moving mechanism which prescribes to him an essentially fixed route of march' (E&S, p. 988). In general, as the material means of production and administration become increasingly centralized, 'discipline inexorably takes over ever larger areas . . . [and] more and more restricts the importance of . . . individually differentiated conduct' (E&S, p. 1156).

Effective control over men and nature rests on calculability—the nexus that links capitalism, formalistic law, and bureaucratic administration. Modern industrial capitalism

> depends upon the possibility of correct calculations. This is true the more capital-intensive industrial capitalism is, and especially the more saturated it is with fixed capital. Industrial capitalism must be able to count on the continuity, trustworthiness and objectivity of the legal order, and on the rational, predictable functioning of legal and administrative agencies. (E&S, p. 1095)

A formalistic legal order, operating 'like a technically rational machine' and thereby enhancing for economic actors 'the possibility of predicting the legal consequences of their action' (E&S, p. 811), is ideally suited to capitalism, as is bureaucratic administration, which satisfies the demand of the capitalistic economy 'that the official business of public administration be discharged precisely, unambiguously, continuously, and with as much speed as possible' (E&S, p. 974).

The calculable, disciplined control over men exercised by capitalism and bureaucracy was established with the (unwitting) help of the ethos of rigorous *self-control* derived from Puritanism. By emphasizing the historical connection between new forms of institutionalized control over men and a new ethos of self-control, between institutionalized discipline and self-discipline, Weber supplements institutional with social psychological analysis in an effort to clarify the relation between social structure and personality.

FORMAL AND SUBSTANTIVE RATIONALITY

In a footnote to the *The Protestant Ethic and the Spirit of Capitalism*, Weber writes: 'a thing is never irrational in itself, but only from a particular ... point of view. For the unbeliever every religious way of life is irrational, for the hedonist every ascetic standard' (PE, p. 194, n. 9). This passage expresses with consummate simplicity two axioms of Weber's social thought. First, rationality does not inhere in things, but is ascribed to them. Secondly, rationality is a relational concept: a thing can be rational (or irrational) only from a particular point of view, never in and of itself.

From the point of view of a given *end*, for example, an action or a pattern of action is rational if it is an efficacious means to the end, and irrational if it is not. A judgment of rationality or irrationality is in this case a judgment about the causal relation—or lack thereof—between an action considered as a means and a given end-in-view. To use Weber's example, an ascetic way of life is rational from the point of view of the end of achievement, but irrational from the point of view of the end of maximizing pleasure.

Alternatively, from the point of view of a given *belief*, an action is rational if it is consistent with the belief, and irrational if it is not. A judgment of rationality or irrationality, in this case, is a judgment about the logical relation—or lack thereof—between action and belief. To return to Weber's example, a religious way of life is rational from the point of view of a belief in the existence of God or an afterlife or in the possibility of salvation through good works, but it is irrational from the point of view of the unbeliever, i.e. from the point of view of the belief that there is no God, no afterlife, and no possibility of salvation through good works.

Weber applies this relational conception of rationality to the analysis of social structure by distinguishing between *formal* and *substantive* rationality. Formal rationality is a matter of fact, substantive rationality a matter of value. Formal rationality refers primarily to the *calculability of means and procedures*, substantive rationality primarily to the *value* (from some explicitly defined standpoint) *of ends or results*. From the point of view of the purely formal objective of maximizing the calculability of action—purely formal because maximally calculable action can be oriented to any of an infinite variety of possible substantive ends—capitalism, science, technology, and the modern legal and administrative system are highly rational. Such purely formal rationality, however, is in perpetual tension with what Weber calls substantive rationality, meaning rationality from the point of view of some particular substantive end, belief, or value commitment.

The distinction between formal and substantive rationality is fundamental to Weber's social thought, linking his empirical analysis of modern society with his moral response to it. The distinction has both methodological and substantive significance. On the methodological plane, it allows Weber to emphasize the value-neutral, purely analytical status of his conception of the rationality of the modern Western social order. Throughout his empirical work, Weber attempts to use richly value-laden terms in a value-neutral manner; rationality is only one of these. Value-neutral conceptions of domination, legitimacy, and charisma are central to his political sociology, as are mysticism, asceticism, prophecy, salvation, and the sacred to his sociology of religion, and duty, meaning, validity, value, culture, conflict and progress to his general conceptual framework. In employing these notions, Weber takes care—especially in *Economy and Society*—to distinguish their value-neutral sociological meanings from their value-laden ordinary meanings. He does the same with 'rationality', divesting the term of the approving connotation it carries in everyday use in order to deploy it as a neutral analytical concept.

The rationality that Weber discerns in modern capitalism, law and bureaucracy, and in the Puritan ethic of vocation that underlies them, is a purely formal rationality.[16] In emphasizing the rationality of the modern social order, Weber is not justifying or defending this social order from a particular value standpoint,[17] but is simply calling attention to social structural and social psychological 'mechanisms' that enhance the calculability of action. Such purely formal rationality is an objective property of the social structure of modern society. However one *evaluates* the increasingly important role of explicit calculation in social life, the *fact* of the growing importance of calculation must be acknowledged. The formal rationality of the modern social order is a matter of fact; whether or not this social order is substantively rational, in contrast, depends on one's point of view—i.e. on the ends, values or beliefs one takes as a standard of rationality.

The substantive significance of Weber's distinction between formal and substantive rationality is twofold. First, the notion of formal rationality underscores what is 'specific and peculiar' about the rationality of the modern Western social order: the fact that the 'end' in terms of which the social order is rationalized—maximum calculability—is not really an end at all but a *generalized means* that indiscriminately facilitates the purposeful pursuit of all substantive ends.[18] To be sure, calculability is not the only element in Weber's conception of the rationality of the modern social order. Weber also stresses the increasing significance of specialized knowledge; the steady erosion of customary, religious and ethical restraints on behavior; the regulation of social life through abstract, general norms; the increasingly instrumental orientation of action in all spheres of social life; the systematic self-control bequeathed to modern society by Puritan asceticism; the devotion to impersonal purposes that defines the ethic of vocation; the development of increasingly powerful techniques for controlling men and nature; and the growing impersonality of relations of power and authority. Yet each of these elements is closely related to calculability and thus to enhanced means–ends rationality; each furthers in a general way the *purposeful, calculated achievement of any and all substantive ends*. Thus technology, to use a hackneyed but nonetheless apposite example, can serve equally to destroy or to maintain human life; progress in technical rationality is embodied equally in increasingly accurate nuclear missiles and in improved kidney dialysis machines. Similarly, purely instrumental action may be devoted just as well to self-enrichment at the expense of others as to the disinterested advancement of a valued cause. These elements of the social structure of modern society can thus be conceived as neutral vehicles for the efficient achievement of any substantive purpose, whatever its significance or 'worth'. It is this substantive neutrality, this indifference to all substantive ends and values, that makes the rationality of the modern Western social order 'specific and peculiar'.

Secondly, and more important, the distinction between formal and substantive rationality serves as a springboard for the exploration of certain tensions inherent in the modern socio-economic order—in particular the tension between the formal rationality of the capitalist economy and its substantive ir-rationality from the point of view of egalitarian, fraternal and caritative values.[19] This antagonism is 'one source of all "social" problems, and above all, of the problems of socialism' (W&G, p. 80; E&S, p. 111). This is because the formal rationality of the modern economic order rests on *institutional foundations that are morally and politically problematic*. Maximum formal rationality, for example, requires the centralized private ownership and control of the means of production (E&S, pp. 138, 161); the ability of owners to hire and fire workers at will and to control the work process (E&S, pp. 128–9, 137–8, 163); thoroughgoing market freedom (E&S, pp. 161–2); and, more generally, the 'struggle of man against man' in the marketplace (E&S, pp. 93, 108). The greater the formal rationality of an economic system—the more closely it approximates what Karl Polanyi (1957) calls a 'system of self-regulating markets'—the more vulnerable such an economic system will be to criticism for its substantive irrationality.

Unsympathetic to socialism, fearing that it would accelerate the bureaucratization of life and bring about 'the dictatorship of the official, not that of the worker' (Soc., p. 209), Weber is none the less sympathetic to socialist criticism of the substantive irrationality of capitalism.[20] He acknowledges that capitalism involves the 'domination of the end (supply meeting demand) by the means' (Soc., p. 202)—in other words the domination of substantive rationality by formal rationality. Maximum formal rationality, for example, in no way guarantees the adequate satisfaction of needs—to take one historically important criterion of substantive rationality. For *needs* may not coincide with *wants*, and it is the latter, ' "awakened" and "directed" by the entrepreneur' through 'aggressive advertising policies' (E&S, pp. 92, 99), that determine what is actually produced. A population may need better health care (according to some—admittedly problematic—criterion of need) but may want more television sets—and in a formally rational economy system more television sets will be produced. Moreover, it is not any and all wants, but only those backed up by purchasing power, that govern production:

> It is not 'demand' (wants) as such, but 'effective demand' for utilities, that . . . regulates the production of goods . . . What is to be produced is thus determined, given the distribution of wealth, by the structure of marginal utilities in the income group that is both inclined and able to purchase a given utility. (W&G, p. 78; E&S, p. 108)

Formal rationality, then, by no means guarantees substantive rationality, at least to the extent that the latter is conceived in terms of adequate provision for needs or wants. For the 'formal rationality of money accounting does not reveal anything about the actual distribution of goods' (E&S, p. 108), and it is the actual distribution of goods that determines whether or not economic production satisfies the needs or wants of a population. Of course 'adequate provision' is itself an ambiguous standard. If it is interpreted as 'the provision of a certain minimum of subsistence for the maximum size of population', then 'the experience of the last few decades would seem to show that formal and substantive rationality coincide to a relatively high degree' (E&S, pp. 108–9). If, on the other hand, adequate provision is interpreted in an egalitarian fashion, or in accordance with the maxim 'to each according to his needs', then formal rationality would appear to work against substantive rationality.

Formal rationality, moreover, is indifferent not only to the substantive demand for adequate provision, but to 'all substantive postulates, an indifference which is absolute if the market is perfectly free'. This perfect indifference to substantive considerations underlies what Weber describes as 'the ultimate limitation, inherent in its very structure, of the rationality of monetary economic calculation' (E&S, p. 108).

A more fundamental criticism of the substantive irrationality of capitalism concerns not the distributional consequences of maximum formal rationality but the inherent nature of formally rational economic activity. Maximum formal rationality, for example, requires the subjection of workers to disciplined control by entrepreneurs and to the inexorable rhythms of factory production (E&S, pp. 108, 138, 1156). Such strict discipline and authoritarian control, regardless of its presumed or actual contribution to individual or collective prosperity, may be rejected from a substantive value standpoint as incompatible with equality and human dignity. More generally, maximum formal rationality 'presupposes the battle of man with man' (E&S, p. 93), the market struggle (*Marktkampf*) of individuals who are formally free but economically compelled to do battle in the marketplace (GEH, p. 277). It is true that 'any human relationship, even the most intimate . . . may involve a struggle with the partner, for instance, over the salvation of his soul' (E&S, p. 636). But the uniquely impersonal *mode* of struggle in the marketplace is 'an abomination to every system of fraternal ethics':

> Where the market is allowed to follow its own autonomous tendencies [i.e. where the market is left unregulated and formal rationality is thereby maximized], its participants do not look toward the persons of each other but only toward the commodity; there are no obligations of brotherliness or reverence, and none of those spontaneous human relations that are sustained by personal unions. (E&S, pp. 636–7)

From an egalitarian or fraternal standpoint, then, capitalism may be considered substantively irrational regardless of the distribution of goods.

If the socialist perspective on capitalism illuminates one dimension of the antagonism between formal and substantive rationality in modern society, a religious perspective illuminates another:

> it is above all the impersonal and economically rationalized (but for this very reason ethically irrational) character of purely commercial relationships that evokes the suspicion . . . of ethical religions. For every purely personal relationship of man to man . . . may be subjected to ethical requirements and ethically regulated. This is true because the structures of these relationships depend upon the individual wills of the participants, leaving room in such relationships for manifestations of the virtue of *caritas*. But this is not the situation in the realm of economically rationalized relationships, where personal control is exercised in inverse ratio to the degree of rational differentiation of the economic structure. There is no possibility, in practice or even in principle, of any caritative regulation of relationships arising between the holder of a savings and loan bank mortgage and the mortgagee who has obtained a loan from the bank, or between a holder of a federal bond and a citizen taxpayer. Nor can any caritative regulation arise in the relationships between stockholders and factory workers, between tobacco importers and foreign plantation workers, or between industrialists and the miners who have dug from the earth the raw materials used in the plants owned by the industrialists. *The growing impersonality of the economy on the basis of association in the marketplace follows its own impersonal laws, disobedience to which entails economic failure and, in the long run, economic ruin.* (W&G, p. 453; E&S, pp. 584–5, emphasis added)

The ideal of *caritas* or brotherly love, 'the foundation of every ecclesiastic ethic, from Islam and Judaism to Buddhism and Christianity' (E&S, p. 1188), is utterly incompatible with formal rationality: this ideal is rendered meaningless in the modern economic realm, since economic action predicated on *caritas* and ignoring the laws of the market is bound in the long run to be self-annihilating.

The antagonism between formal and substantive rationality may thus be interpreted as a tension between conflicting values: between calculability, efficiency and impersonality on the one hand and fraternity, equality and *caritas* on the other. This is an example of what Weber calls 'value-interpretation' (*Wertinterpretation*)—a mode of analysis that

> teaches us to 'understand' the intellectual, psychological, and spiritual [*geistigen*] content of [the object under study]; it develops and raises to the level of explicit 'evaluation' that which we 'feel' dimly and vaguely. For this purpose, interpretation is not at all required to enunciate or to 'suggest' a *value judgment*. What it actually 'suggests' in the course of analysis are rather various possible *relationships of the object to values[Wertbeziehungen des Objektes]*. (M, p. 143)

The idea of an irreconcilable opposition between formal and substantive rationality is the guiding thread of Weber's 'value-interpretation' of the modern socio-economic order, suggesting 'various possible relationships of the object [modern capitalism] to values'. To sum these up in a phrase: characterized by a high degree of formal rationality, the modern capitalist economic order maximizes the values of calculability, efficiency and impersonality but is deeply inhospitable to egalitarian, fraternal and caritative values.

Weber interprets the tension between formal and substantive rationality not only as an abstract axiological tension, a tension between conflicting values, but also as a real social tension, a tension between competing interests and between the groups that are the bearers of these interests. Formal rationality is a value-neutral concept, but the formal rationality of the modern social and economic order is *not* neutral with respect to the values and interests of different social groups. Maximum formal rationality favors economically powerful groups—those with monopolistic or quasi-monopolistic price-setting powers, with the power to 'dictate the terms of exchange to contractual partners' (E&S, p. 214). Thus freedom of contract, a prime condition of maximum formal rationality, is a formally neutral institution, but it is not neutral in practice. For it in effect guarantees to economically advantaged groups the opportunity to use their superior economic resources 'without legal restraints as a means of achieving power over others' (W&G, p. 562; E&S, p. 730). Nor is the principle of formal legal equality neutral in its consequences:

> The propertyless masses ... are not served by the formal
> 'equality before the law' and the 'calculable' adjudication and
> administration demanded by bourgeois interests. Naturally, in
> their eyes justice and administration should serve to equalize
> their economic and social life-opportunities [*Lebenschancen*]
> in the face of the propertied classes. Justice and administration
> can fulfill this function only if they assume a character that is
> informal because 'ethical' with respect to substantive content.
> (E&S, p. 980)

Formal rationality in the economic and legal spheres thus favors
some groups at the expense of others. As a result, economically
privileged groups deriving their power from market transactions
have a strong interest in maximizing formal rationality, while
economically threatened or disprivileged groups have an equally
strong interest in subjecting economic life to substantive regulation and thus in reducing formal rationality.

The tension between formal and substantive rationality, then,
is both a tension between conflicting values and a tension
between social groups with divergent interests: between groups
interested in and benefiting from calculability and efficiency on
the one hand and groups interested in and benefiting from the
substantive regulation of social and economic life on the other.[21]
This tension is expressed most dramatically in the political
struggle over socialism; but it also finds expression in all attempts
to increase or decrease the substantive regulation of social and
economic life. Indeed, the tension between formal and substantive rationality is at the root of many of the great political
conflicts of our time. Even today, many advanced industrial
societies, most notably England and the United States, are torn
by bitter conflicts between groups wishing to curb the substantive
regulation of economic life in order to restore a lost capitalistic
paradise of unimpeded formal rationality and groups wishing to
extend the substantive regulation of the social and economic
order.

THE IDEA OF A RATIONAL SOCIETY

The modern Western social order, in Weber's diagnosis, is
highly, indeed uniquely rational. But it is rational only from a

purely formal point of view, only in a 'specific and peculiar', narrowly restricted sense that excludes the evaluative resonance traditionally carried by the word 'rational'. It is a social order founded on the 'dominion of conscienceless reason', to use the suggestive phrase of Benjamin Nelson (1971, p. 169). The disjunction between reason and conscience—between formal and substantive rationality—is unique to modern society. Never, in premodern times, had social and economic life been regulated by mechanisms so relentlessly indifferent to substantive ends and values; never before had means and procedures become so completely autonomous, so thoroughly divorced from ends.

If 'rational' is used with the narrowly circumscribed meaning that Weber assigns to the expression 'formally rational', then a rational social life is no mere possibility, but the inescapable fate of the modern world. But what if 'rational' is understood in its traditional, broadly evaluative sense? Is a *substantively* rational society possible? This question, a concern of social theorists from Plato through Marx, is for Weber an extra-scientific one, answerable only from the point of view of a particular value commitment in terms of which the meaning of substantive rationality is defined. According to Weber, there is no scientific way of reconciling opposed value commitments and, consequently, no scientific way of reconciling conflicting definitions of substantive rationality.

Weber's analysis of Western rationalism, like his social thought in general, does have a critical edge. He demonstrates the extreme inhospitality of the modern formally rational social and economic order to the values of equality, fraternity and *caritas*, and he shows how formal rationality furthers the interests of economically privileged groups. But the critical impulse in his sociological work is exclusively diagnostic: unlike Marx and Durkheim, Weber nowhere suggests a therapy (Löwith, 1982, p. 25). The limits Weber imposes on the critical functions of sociological analysis derive from his conception of the inherent limits of any form of scientific inquiry. Like the Western social order as a whole, science is a rational enterprise only in a purely formal sense, and the limits of science are a special case of the limits of formal rationality. Science, because its rationality is purely formal, is incapable of yielding value judgments, incapable of arbitrating between conflicting value commitments, incapable of defining substantive rationality, and incapable, finally, of supporting a conception of the good society. It is this notion of the limits of objective, scientific rationality that I explore in the next chapter.

NOTES TO CHAPTER 1

1 This essay appears in English as the 'Author's Introduction' in Talcott Parsons's translation of *The Protestant Ethic and the Spirit of Capitalism*. It should be emphasized, though, that it is not part of *The Protestant Ethic*.

2 Weber's two main bodies of empirical work—his comparative historical studies in the sociology of religion and his vast sociological *summa, Economy and Society*—were both left unfinished at his death. Besides these works, Weber produced technically sophisticated specialized studies on ancient Roman agrarian history, the social structure of ancient Mediterranean society, medieval trading companies, the development of Western music, the modern stock exchange, contemporary East German agriculture, and the industrial psychology of a textile factory (FMW, pp. 9–23; Bendix, 1962, p. 469).

3 For comprehensive and penetrating analyses of the thematic coherence of Weber's empirical work, see Bendix (1962) and Schluchter (1981). Others who have urged attention to the universal–historical perspective that underlies and informs Weber's empirical work include Mommsen (1965, 1974), Nelson (1973, 1974, 1976), and Tenbruck (1980).

4 *Economy and Society* (Part One, ch. 2) contains Weber's most extensive— and most difficult—discussion of the rationality of modern capitalism. See especially sections 1–14, 22, 25, 30, 31 and 41. The discussion in GEH (esp. chs 22, 27 and 30) is more accessible, but considerably less detailed. Good discussions of Weber's theory of capitalism, emphasizing his conception of the institutional underpinnings of economic rationality, can be found in Parsons (1947, pp. 30–55) and Collins (1980).

5 It is important to distinguish Weber's ideal-typical conception of purely rational market exchange from the actual course of exchange in the market, which always diverges to some extent from the ideal type, approaching it only as a limiting case. In reality, market exchange has seldom been free of traditional, conventional, or legal restrictions, and market transactions have seldom been purely *zweckrational*. Weber argues, however, that market exchange becomes increasingly rational as a capitalist economy develops (E&S, pp. 638–9). Moreover, such monopolistic restraints on market freedom as do develop in a capitalist economy differ radically from traditional restraints 'by their purely economic and rational character': the power of the monopolist rests upon 'an entirely calculated mastery of market conditions' (E&S, p. 639). The rationality of market exchange, in short, is an ideal-typical construct, but one increasingly approximated by reality. Weber makes this point explicitly with respect to another ideal-typical construct, the theory of marginal utility. 'The historical particularity of the capitalist epoch, and . . . the significance of the theory of marginal utility for the understanding of this epoch, lies in the fact that . . . *the approximation of*

reality to the propositions of this theory has been constantly increasing'
(GAW, p. 371; MU, p. 33; emphasis added). Just as life may imitate art, so
social reality may approximate the ideal-typical constructions of social
theory.

6	Donald Levine (1981a, 1982) argues persuasively that a distinction between
subjective and objectified rationality is implicit in Weber's work and helpful
in interpreting that work, as well as the work of Simmel and Parsons.

7	Weber's conception of the formal rationality of law, though relatively
neglected (in comparison with the rationality of capitalism or bureaucracy)
by most commentators, is arguably the 'core of [his] substantive sociology'
(Parsons, 1971, p. 40). For a thorough analysis of Weber's conception of the
emergence of legal rationality in the West, see Bendix (1962, ch. 12). And
for an interesting analysis of the relation between Weber's conception of the
rationality of law and his conception of the rationality of other institutional
spheres, see Schluchter (1981, ch. 5).

8	Weber's conception of rational bureaucratic administration, like his con-
ceptions of formalistic law and industrial capitalism, is an ideal type: it is a
selective accentuation of certain especially significant aspects of reality, not
a faithful 'copy' of reality. As Wolfgang Mommsen (1974, p. 19) has
remarked, 'The "ideal type" of bureaucracy was deliberately designed by
Weber in such a way as to underline those elements which he considered
particularly relevant in regard to the future destinies of the individualistic,
liberal societies of the West'. Mommsen's book is a provocative exploration
of the theme of bureaucratic rationalization in Weber's political sociology
and political philosophy. For a closely reasoned account of Weber's conception of the nature and limits of bureaucratic rationality, see Beetham (1974,
ch. 3).

9	Today, of course, bureaucratic administration is more likely to be assailed
for its *inefficiency* than praised for its efficiency. Still, in comparison with
what Weber calls 'administration by dilettantes'—meaning any non-formal
mode of administration by non-experts—bureaucracy is indeed efficient. It
is this comparative efficiency, not an absolute efficiency, that Weber
emphasizes.

In other respects, however, Weber anticipates many of the ideas of later
critics of bureaucracy. He argues, for example, that the development of the
state bureaucracy stifled capitalism in the Roman Empire, and suggests that
a similar 'choking-off of private economic initiative by the bureaucracy' (S
Tr, p. 313) might well occur again. Unchecked bureaucratic rationalization,
moreover, threatens not only economic initiative but personal freedom: the
'casing of the new serfdom [*Gehäuse für die neue Hörigkeit*]', Weber warns,
is already visible (S Tr, pp. 281–2; cf. E&S, pp. 1401–3).

10	On the notion of breakthrough in Weber's work, see Parsons (1963, pp.
xxix–xxxv); Nelson (1973); and Schluchter (1981, ch. 6).

11	This is a classic example of what Weber means by an 'ideal interest'. (See
FMW, p. 280, where he argues that man's conduct is governed not by ideas,
but by 'material and ideal interests'.)

12	The fact that 'continuous work has become a necessary part of [men's] lives
. . . expresses what is, from the view-point of personal happiness, so irrational about this sort of life, where a man exists for the sake of his business, instead of the reverse' (PE, p. 70; cf. pp. 53, 78).

13	The worldly asceticism of the Puritans represents one mode of religio-
ethical rationality, but by no means the only one. The Confucian ethic of

harmonious adjustment to the world, by virtue of its 'practical turn of mind', its utilitarian orientation, and its emphasis on 'watchful . . . self-control' (R Ch, pp. 228, 241), equally deserves to be called rational. Even world-rejecting Buddhism is rational, producing 'a constantly alert control of all natural instinctive drives' (E&S, p. 627). This is true despite the fact that Buddhism regards 'all rational purposive activity . . . as leading away from salvation, except of course the subjective activity of concentrated contemplation, which empties the soul of the passion for life and every connection with worldly interests' (E&S, p. 628). In his extensive writings on religion, Weber explores the affinities and disaffinities between different paths of religious rationalization and the rationalization of economic conduct (cf. FMW, p. 293). His conclusion, expounded in rather sweeping terms in R Ch (pp. 226–49) and S Tr (pp. 192–205), is that religious rationalization in the West promoted economic rationalization, while religious rationalization in the East—particularly in China and India—hindered economic rationalization.

14 The contribution of Puritanism to the development of capitalism, Weber writes, 'instructs us in the paradox of unintended consequences [*die Paradoxie der Wirkung gegenüber dem Wollen*]; i.e. the relation of man and fate, of what he intended by his acts as against what actually came of them' (GAR, p. 524; R Ch, p. 238).

15 For a discussion—and criticism—of Weber's conception of rationality, emphasizing the theme of control, see Marcuse (1971).

16 In this and the following paragraph, I use the notion of formal rationality in a somewhat broader and more general sense than Weber does. Weber distinguishes between the formal and substantive rationality of economic action (E&S, pp. 85–6, 93–4, 105–11, 118, 128, 138, 140, 160–4), law (E&S, pp. 655–7, 809–31, 880–95), and administration (E&S, pp. 226, 239–40, 269–70; FMW, pp. 298–9), but he does not explicitly generalize the concept of formal rationality to characterize the modern Western social order as a whole.

17 Weber's claim to employ value-free concepts in his empirical work has been more often attacked than understood. As is clear from his political writings and from his impassioned lectures on 'Science as a Vocation' and 'Politics as a Vocation', Weber harbors intense, though ultimately ambivalent, attitudes toward the rationality of modern civilization. (I discuss these attitudes in relation to Weber's moral vision in my final chapter.) These personal attitudes, however, do not impugn the value-neutrality of his descriptive emphasis on the rationality of modern civilization. To say that Weber's characterization of modern civilization in terms of its 'specific and peculiar rationalism' is value-neutral simply means that this characterization embodies neither positive nor negative value judgments about modern civilization. But while it involves no *value judgments*, Weber's emphasis on the rationality of modern civilization is nonetheless constructed *in relation to values*. Considerations of value-relevance (*Wertbeziehung*) guide the formulation of his conception of modern civilization, determining which aspects of the infinity of empirical reality are selected as significant and molded into a coherent concept. The elements selected for their significance may be related positively, negatively, or in both ways to values—and the values to which they are related may themselves be diverse and even contradictory, encompassing not only the personal values of the investigator but the values of his community and of his age as well. Unless a concept is

formed through the investigator's consistent selection of features that he personally prizes or abhors—and this is manifestly not the case for Weber's nuanced and complex conception of Western rationalism—the concept cannot be said to be inherently value-laden. The value-relevance of Weber's conception of Western rationalism, in short, is perfectly compatible with its value-neutrality—and Weber makes this quite explicit through his distinction between formal and substantive rationality.

18 This theme, implicit in Weber's work, is developed explicitly in the work of his friend and contemporary Georg Simmel, particularly in *The Philosophy of Money* (1978).

19 The substantive irrationality of what Weber calls formal rationality has been stressed by Löwith (1982) and Marcuse (1971). Perceptive remarks on the tension between formal and substantive rationality can also be found in Parsons (1947, pp. 35–55); Mommsen (1974, pp. 65–71); and Beetham (1974, pp. 273–5).

20 See Mommsen (1974, ch. 3) for a good discussion of Weber's attitude towards socialism.

21 Of course there are also tensions and conflicts among groups interested in the substantive regulation of the social order—conflicts over the particular substantive ends to be furthered and over the appropriate manner of pursuing shared ends.

2

The Nature and Limits of Rational Action

Underlying Weber's conception of the rationality of the modern social order is a conception of the rationality of individual action. And just as there are inherent limits to the rationality of the modern social order, so, according to Weber, there are inherent limits to the rationality of individual action. I explore those limits in this chapter, shifting from the perspective of historical sociology to that of philosophical psychology, from a macroscopic focus on the broad outlines of modern society to a microscopic focus on the anatomy of rational action.

Weber's conception of rational action is not easily pinned down. One reason for its elusiveness is that Weber does not aim to specify once and for all what is rational and what is not, but aims rather to bring out the manysidedness (*Vielseitigkeit*) of the concept of rational action (GAR, p. 35, n. 1; PE, p. 194, n. 9). Compounding the difficulty of grasping Weber's meaning is the terse, undeveloped, fragmentary character of his remarks on rational action. These remarks, finally, scattered throughout his methodological writings, are not easily reconciled with one another, for Weber develops different conceptions of rational action, draws different distinctions, and uses different terminology in different contexts.

Three distinctions drawn by Weber are examined in this chapter. The first is a very general distinction between non-rational and rational conduct—between spontaneous, instinctive, habitual or otherwise unreflective conduct and deliberate, consciously guided action. The second, corresponding to the structural tension between formal and substantive rationality, is the famous distinction between *zweckrational* action, oriented to calculable expectations, and *wertrational* action, oriented to consciously upheld values. The third, and most important, distinction is between subjective and objective rationality—the former depending on the inner orientation of the actor, the latter on the extent to which action measures up to an objective standard. The chapter concludes with a discussion of the limits of objective rationality.

RATIONAL AND NON-RATIONAL ACTION

Weber's most famous discussion of rational action occurs in the opening pages of *Economy and Society*. Here he sketches four ways in which action may be 'determined' (*bestimmt*). Traditional action is determined by longstanding habits; affectual action, by strong feelings; *wertrational* action, by a conscious belief in the intrinsic value of acting in a certain way, regardless of the consequences of so acting; and *zweckrational* action, by a consciously calculating attempt to achieve desired ends with appropriate means.

Underlying this four-fold typology is a more basic, though implicit, distinction between rational and non-rational action. In so far as the individual is not the self-conscious and deliberate author of his action, in so far as he is carried along by habit (as in purely traditional action) or carried away by feeling (as in purely affectual action)—to this extent, his conduct is non-rational. In so far as the individual acts deliberately and is consciously aware of what he is doing, on the other hand, his action is rational (in the most inclusive sense of this word). In reality, of course, the transition between purely non-rational and purely rational actions is continuous, and the vast majority of all concrete action falls somewhere between the two extremes of unreflective, quasi-automatic reaction to stimuli and deliberate, consciously planned action. Weber underscores the gradual nature of the transition by remarking that both traditional and affectual action may become rationalized, may shade over into one or the other form of rational action. Traditional ways of acting may be more or less consciously upheld; emotional impulses may be sublimated to varying degrees and consciously channeled in a certain direction (E&S, p. 25).

In general, Weber suggests, action is becoming increasingly

rational in this most inclusive sense of the word: in a growing range of situations, action tends to be deliberate and self-conscious rather than unquestioningly traditional or blindly emotional. But if social action is increasingly rational, it is *not* predominantly rational (E&S, p. 7). The subjective rationality of individual action does not typically progress *pari passu* with the objectified, supra-individual rationality of the social structure (Categ., pp. 178–9). Even in a highly rationalized social order, most action takes place 'in a state of inarticulate half-consciousness or actual unconsciousness of its subjective meaning . . . [and] is governed by impulse or habit' (E&S, p. 21).

WERTRATIONAL AND *ZWECKRATIONAL* ACTION

Weber is less interested in distinguishing different *degrees* of rationality than he is in specifying different *kinds* of rationality—different ways in which action may be deliberately and consciously guided. Thus he distinguishes between *wertrational* and *zweckrational* action—the former directed towards the realization of some value believed to be *inherent in* a certain way of acting, the latter toward the achievement of some end or ends that are expected to *result from* a certain way of acting. *Wertrational* action is oriented to an act's intrinsic properties, *zweckrational* action to its anticipated and intended consequences. *Wertrational* action presupposes a conscious belief about the intrinsic value or inherent rightness of a certain way of acting, *zweckrational* action conscious reasoning in terms of means and ends.

Consider the following medical scenario:

a transplant surgeon detects signs of tissue rejection in a patient who has just received a donor kidney. The surgeon is virtually certain that within a week the kidney will have to be surgically removed and the patient transferred to dialysis equipment again. Although in no immediate clinical danger, the patient is suffering from postoperative depression. It is altogether possible that if the patient is told at this time that the transplant appears to be a failure, his depression will become more severe. This, in turn, might lead to a worsening of the patient's physical condition, perhaps even to a life-threatening extent (Munson, 1979, p. 173).

If the surgeon tells his patient the truth about his condition, acting on the basis of a conscious conviction that truthfulness is an unconditional obligation, his action is *wertrational*. If, on the other hand, he deceives the patient, believing deception to be necessary in order to prevent a dangerous relapse, his action is *zweckrational*. The action is deliberate and consciously guided in both cases—but by fundamentally different sorts of reasons. One reason appeals to the intrinsic rightness of truth-telling as such, regardless of its consequences; the other appeals to the detrimental consequences of telling this particular patient the truth at this particular time, and to the beneficial consequences of temporarily concealing the truth from him. Weber's two types of rational action, then, correspond to two sorts of reasons for acting in a particular way: reasons that invoke value postulates, and reasons that invoke anticipated consequences.

It is of course the *zweckrational* orientation, not the *wertrational* orientation, that Weber conceives as increasingly salient in modern society. *Zweckrational* action appears in its purest form in economic exchange, but conduct in every sphere of life is increasingly (though far from exclusively) *zweckrational*—increasingly oriented to more or less consciously held expectations about the consequences of prospective ways of acting.[1] Underlying this salience of *zweckrational* action are certain structural features of modern society—features that increase the calculability (in Weber's terminology, the formal rationality) of action in the economic, legal and administrative realms. This structurally conditioned calculability, discussed in some detail in Chapter 1, extends the possibilities of *zweckrational* action by enlarging the domain of prospective actions about which reliable expectations can be formed. There are limits, though, to the expanding significance of *Zweckrationalität*. Weber notes that a pattern of social interaction 'based *solely* on *zweckrational* motives' is in general far less stable than one resting on longstanding custom or on feelings of obligation, particularly those engendered by a belief in the 'legitimacy' of some 'order' (*Ordnung*) (W&G, p. 23; E&S, p. 31).

SUBJECTIVE AND OBJECTIVE RATIONALITY

Both *Wertrationalität* and *Zweckrationalität* are defined *subjectively*—i.e. from the point of view of the actor. *Wertrational* action is defined by the actor's subjective belief in the intrinsic value of a particular way of acting, and by his conscious effort to act in accordance with this belief. The objective 'correctness' of the actor's belief—assuming for the moment that this correctness could be established—has nothing to do with the subjective rationality of the action. *Zweckrational* action, too, is defined subjectively, by the actor's expectations about the consequences of alternative ways of acting, and by his conscious effort to bring about one or some of these expected consequences. Again, the objective correctness of his expectations is irrelevant to the subjective rationality of his action.

Wertrational and *zweckrational* action, then, are rational only from the subjective point of view of the actor. Such purely subjective rationality needs to be sharply distinguished from what Weber calls 'objectively correct rationality' (*objektive Richtigkeitsrationalität*; GAW, p. 408; Categ., p. 154)—from action that 'uses the objectively correct means in accordance with scientific knowledge' (M, p. 34). As an advocate and practitioner of interpretive (*verstehende*) sociology, committed to explaining social phenomena in terms of the subjective meaning of individual action, Weber is primarily interested in the forms and functions of subjective rationality. In *Economy and Society*, for example, he examines the way in which complex social structures such as markets, bureaucracies and systems of law depend on the subjectively *zweckrational* or *wertrational* (as well as traditional or affectual) orientations of individual actors. But as a philosopher, committed to specifying the relation between scientific knowledge and human action, he is interested in the nature and limits of objective rationality. It is these limits that I discuss in the remainder of this chapter.[2]

The province of objective rationality is narrower than that of subjective rationality: there is an objectively rational correlate of subjectively *zweckrational* but not of subjectively *wertrational* action. The selection of means to a given end can be assessed in terms of its objective rationality, since it is possible to discriminate objectively—for Weber, scientifically—between adequate and inadequate means. But the notion of objective rationality does not apply to *wertrational* action—to action conceived as intrinsically rather than as instrumentally valuable, as an end in itself rather than as means to some further end. This is because the value postulates to which *wertrational* action is oriented, unlike the expectations (about consequences) to which *zweckrational* action is oriented, cannot be objectively assessed. Such value postulates embody knowledge (*Erkenntnis*), but it is knowledge of what ought to be (*des Seinsollenden*), not of what is (*des Seienden*) (GAW, p. 148; M, p. 51). The former, according to Weber, is essentially subjective; only the latter can be objectively valid.

The distinction between subjective and objective rationality, then, applies only to *zweckrational* action. This distinction can be clarified by considering the categories 'means' and 'ends'. They are at the same time categories of subjective experience—part of the conceptual scheme of the *zweckrational* actor—and categories of objective analysis—part of the conceptual scheme of the scientific observer. To the actor, these categories facilitate the prospective planning of action; to the observer, they facilitate its retrospective explanation or evaluation. Subjective rationality pertains to the actor's use of these categories, objective rationality to the observer's.[3]

Whether or not an action is subjectively rational depends on the actor's self-understanding. To the extent that he conceives of his prospective action in a means–ends framework and chooses means he believes to be adequate to some clearly perceived end, his action is subjectively rational, regardless of whether or not his means are in fact adequate. It is the *perceived* appropriateness of the means, not their *actual* appropriateness, that makes action subjectively rational. Much magical conduct, Weber notes, is subjectively rational (M, p. 34); magical practices are often carried out in the belief that they will contribute to the realization of certain consciously pursued ends.

Whether or not an action is objectively rational, in contrast, depends on the judgment of a scientific observer—i.e. one who is able to ascertain empirically the appropriateness of the actor's conduct as a means to some end. This end may be the one intended by the actor, or it may be one of which the actor is unaware but toward which his conduct in fact tends. Subjectively rational action may be objectively irrational: magical means, for example, may be objectively unrelated to the ends they are intended to further. Conversely, subjectively non-rational action—action that is not conceived by the actor as purposefully directed toward the realization of some end—may be objectively rational from the point of view of some unintended or unacknowledged end. (The search for such latent objective rationality is characteristic of psychoanalysis—witness Freud's concept of the 'advantage through illness' (1953, p. 391; 1963, p. 196)—and of functional analysis in sociology.)

THE LIMITS OF OBJECTIVE RATIONALITY

The notions of subjective and objective rationality differ markedly in their implications: subjective rationality is a purely descriptive, objective rationality an inherently normative concept. Imputations of subjective rationality are value-neutral characterizations, while imputations of objective rationality are evaluative appraisals. No value judgment is involved in characterizing an action as subjectively rational. A subjectively rational action is simply one that has a certain type of subjective meaning—a meaning formulable in terms of means and ends and more or less explicitly formulated in such terms by the actor. Imputations of objective rationality, in contrast, are inherently evaluative, for an objectively rational action is by definition one that uses the 'correct' means of attaining some end. Because judgments of objective rationality have strong normative connotations, it is important to specify more precisely the circumstances in which such judgments can legitimately be made.

All subjectively *zweckrational* action involves conscious reckoning in terms of means and ends. Such reckoning, however, may have a narrower or a wider scope, depending on whether the actor has in mind a single clearly defined end or a number of possible alternative ends. In the former case, the actor adopts a *technical* point of view, and calculation is limited to the weighing of alternative means to a fixed and given end. In the latter case, he adopts what Weber calls an *economic* point of view, and calculation extends to the weighing of alternative ends and unintended but foreseeable secondary consequences as well as means. Choosing what means to employ, given a fixed and unambiguous end, is a technical problem; choosing what ends to pursue and what means to employ, given a stock of resources, is an economic problem (E&S, pp. 65–7).

Whenever action is conceived by the actor exclusively as a means to some more or less clearly defined end, this action can be understood as a *technique* (E&S, p. 65). This is true regardless of the substantive content of the end. There are techniques, as Weber says, of 'every conceivable type of action' (E&S, p. 65): techniques for achieving ideal as well as material ends, trivial as well as significant ends, ends that are widely regarded as reprehensible as well as those universally believed to be valuable.

While every technique is by definition subjectively rational, techniques vary widely in their degree of objective rationality. At what Weber calls the 'highest level of [objective] rationality' (E&S, p. 65), the techniques for achieving given ends are determined in accordance with scientific knowledge. This is an important idea, for it implies that the most rational means for attaining given ends can be determined scientifically, hence objectively. But it is also, as Weber recognizes, a problematic idea.

The capacity of science to serve as an objective arbiter of the rationality of action is in fact narrowly limited. The problem is not simply that there are limits to scientific knowledge, in particular to knowledge of social phenomena, and that, as a result, it may be impossible to predict with confidence and precision whether or not a given end will be achieved by employing certain means. For even perfect knowledge of the consequences of alternative ways of acting would not automatically engender objective judgments of the 'most rational' way of achieving a given end. It is true that perfect knowledge would enable one to characterize certain means (those incapable of bringing about or unlikely to bring about the desired end) as objectively irrational and others (those certain or highly likely to bring about the desired end) as objectively rational—from a purely technical point of view. It would not, however, enable one to choose the 'most rational' of two alternative means, both certain (or equally likely) to bring about the desired end, but differing considerably in their secondary (unintended but foreseeable) consequences, for there is no objective way of assessing the 'value' of the secondary consequences.

Moreover, common sense dictates that an action may be irrational even if its technique is objectively rational—even if the means employed are certain or highly likely to bring about some desired end. Undesirable secondary consequences ('side effects') may outweigh the value of the end, or (even in the absence of negative side effects), the cost of the means may be too high relative to the value of the end. Such an action would be (objectively) rational from the narrow technical point of view, but (subjectively) irrational from the broader economic point of view.

Judgments of objective rationality can be made only from the technical point of view, not from the economic point of view. For when an actor adopts the economic point of view, he does not simply calculate the technical adequacy of alternative means to a single given end. Instead, his calculations are oriented to a variety of possible ends, and to the fact that he controls a limited stock of resources that can be used to realize some of these ends. His problem is to select the combination of means and ends that will maximize his 'utility'. To the extent that he is guided by conscious calculations about ends, means and secondary consequences, his action is subjectively rational. But it cannot be objectively rational, for there is no objective way of assessing the comparative importance of alternative possible ends or of balancing desirable ends against undesirable secondary consequences.

Technical rationality, then, can be measured against an objective standard: scientific knowledge of means-ends relations. Economic rationality, in contrast, is purely subjective: the conscious calculations about the comparative value of ends, means, and secondary consequences that make action economically rational cannot be assessed in terms of their objective correctness. Objective rationality, in short, exists only in the sphere of technique.

This does not diminish the significance of objective rationality. Technical problems can be solved in an objectively rational manner, and technical progress—the progressive subordination of nature to human purposes, guided by an ever-expanding stock of scientific knowledge—has transformed and continues to transform our civilization. Moreover, not only the material world, but the social world as well—including the 'political, social, educational, and propagandistic manipulation and domination of human beings' (M, p. 35)—is subject to technical rationalization.

Most important problems of social life, however, even those that have an important technical dimension, are not purely technical problems—i.e. problems of finding the most rational means to a fixed and precisely specified end. Problems of social policy, in particular, are seldom purely technical. There may *seem* to be 'general agreement about the self-evident character of certain goals ... [including] the concrete problems of social hygiene, poor relief, factory inspection' (M, pp. 55–6). This illusion of self-evidence, however, is shattered when one of these seemingly noncontroversial goals becomes the object of social policy, and it is discovered that 'each individual understood something quite different by the ostensibly unambiguous end' (M, p. 12). Consider a contemporary example. There is general agreement in the United States that the health of textile manufacturing workers ought to be protected by federal legislation. In addition, there is general agreement about the effects of various types of protective equipment on workers' health. Yet this problem does not have a technically rational solution, for the goal—protecting workers' health—is only apparently unambiguous. Should health be protected to the maximum extent *technically* feasible? Or to the extent *economically* feasible (up to the point that the cost of protective equipment would threaten the viability of the industry)? Or to the extent that the benefits of better health outweigh the costs of protective equipment? And in this case, how are the benefits of better health to be estimated in monetary terms? What is the money value of a 5 percent decrease in deaths from Brown Lung Disease? Clearly this is not a technical problem at all: agreement on the general goal of protecting workers' health masks disagreement over the

interpretation of this goal—i.e. over what the specific objective
of government policy should be.

Scientific knowledge can determine 'what is to be done' only
when an unambiguous end is given and when there is an unambiguous way of comparing the rationality of alternative means of
achieving the given end. In Weber's view, the most pressing
problems of practical social life—problems of economic and
social policy—do not meet these criteria: they 'cannot be resolved merely on the basis of purely technical considerations
which assume already settled ends. Normative standards of
value can and must be the objects of *dispute* in a discussion of a
problem of social policy because the problem lies in the domain
of general *cultural* values' (M, p. 56).

This does not mean that science has no role in solving such
problems. On the contrary, one of the basic functions of social
science, according to Weber, is to establish reliable empirical
knowledge that can be taken into account by policy-makers. But
science cannot dictate a 'solution' to problems of social policy:
the decision will inevitably be based on values, not on
knowledge.

> Even such simple questions as the extent to which an end
> should sanction unavoidable means, or the extent to which
> undesired repercussions should be taken into consideration
> . . . are entirely matters of choice or compromise. There is no
> (rational or empirical) scientific procedure of any kind what-
> soever which can provide us with a decision here. (M, pp.
> 18–19)

Weber's conception of the limits of objective rationality recalls
Hume's strictures on the practical impotence of reason. 'Reason
alone', Hume writes in *A Treatise of Human Nature*, 'can never
be a motive to any action of the will' (p. 413). From the point of
view of its relation to action, reason is 'perfectly inert', exercising
'no influence on our passions and actions' (pp. 457–8). Hume
concludes that 'reason is, and ought only to be the slave of the
passions, and can never pretend to any other office than to serve
and obey them' (p. 415). In the Weberian idiom, reason is the
slave of human values and of the ends people choose to pursue by
virtue of holding certain values—values for which no rational

justification can be given. These values, according to Weber, are in eternal conflict with one another, and this conflict cannot be rationally resolved. It is this conception of value conflict—a conception that underlies Weber's persistent emphasis on the limits of rationality—that I examine in Chapter 3.

NOTES TO CHAPTER 2

1 'On the whole, the course of historical development involves ... a steady advance of the *zweckrational* ordering of consensual action by means of rational rules, and in particular the progressive transformation of informal associations [*Verbänden*] into institutions organized on an instrumentally rational basis [*zweckrational geordnete Anstalten*]' (GAW, pp. 446–7; Categ., p. 177).

2 The expression 'objective rationality', as Donald Levine has remarked (1981a, p. 11), is ambiguous, denoting objective correctness or validity on the one hand and supra-individual, institutionalized rationality on the other. My concern in this chapter is with objective rationality in the former sense; pp. 9–23 of Chapter 1 examine objective rationality in the latter sense (what Levine calls 'objectified rationality').

3 Actor and observer, it should be noted, may use the categories means and ends in different ways to make sense of the same concrete course of action. In particular, the end imputed to an action by an observer may not coincide with the end consciously intended by the actor.

3

The Ethical Irrationality
of the World*

Weber's conception of the limits of rationality is rooted in his understanding of value conflict. If, as Weber argues, value conflict cannot be reconciled, then the scope of rational decision-making is narrowly limited. Only in situations shielded from value conflict can choice be rational; between conflicting value commitments, choice must be arbitrary. Furthermore, if value conflict is irreconcilable, then conflicting conceptions of substantive rationality, based on conflicting value commitments, are likewise irreconcilable, and the ideal of a substantively rational society—of a 'good society'—is meaningless from a scientific point of view, since there is no rational way to reconcile conflicting conceptions of the nature of a substantively rational society. The claim that value conflict cannot be reconciled, in short, is the basis for Weber's argument that there are inherent limits to the rationality of individual action and to the rationality of the social order.

This chapter explores the philosophical and sociological foundations of Weber's claim that value conflict is irreconcilable. Its perspective is expository, not critical.[1] Exposition, in this case, has its own risks: the highly elliptical character of Weber's remarks requires us to go beyond straight exegesis in an attempt to reconstruct his theory of value conflict from a handful of tantalizingly sketchy passages.

Weber uses a rich variety of language, much of it uncharacteristically extravagant, to express his conception of value conflict. He speaks, for example, of the 'struggle that the gods of the various orders and values are engaged in' (FMW, p. 148); of

*The title is taken from 'Politics as a Vocation' (FMW, p. 122).

'absolute polytheism' as the only appropriate methaphysic of the world of value (M, p. 17; FMW, p. 147); of an 'irreconcilable death-struggle' between values (M, p. 17); of the 'various life-spheres, each of which is governed by different laws' (FMW, p. 123); of the 'infinite multiplicity of evaluative attitudes' (M, p. 144); of the conflict between ethics and 'autonomous, extra-ethical' value spheres (M, p. 17); of the clash between 'ultimate *Weltanschauungen*' (FMW, p. 117); and of the 'ethical ir-rationality of the world' (FMW, p. 122).

The metaphorical richness of Weber's language makes it hard to specify exactly what he means by value conflict. I shall argue that two distinct conceptions of value conflict can be discerned in his work, deriving from two distinct conceptions of value. Value is conceived on the one hand as subjective, as embodied in *value-orientations* that are created by individuals, and on the other hand as objective, as embodied in *value spheres* that exist independently of individuals. Similarly, value conflict is conceived on one level as a contingent conflict between the subjective value-orientations of individuals and, on another level, as a necessary conflict between objective, supra-individual value spheres. Consider these two conceptions in turn.

THE CLASH OF VALUE-ORIENTATIONS

Value-orientations are not particular value judgments but *Weltanschauungen*—'general views of life and the universe', as Shils and Finch (M, p. 57) translate this untranslatable term.[2] Simultaneously theoretical and practical, they endow the world with meaning and at the same time define paths of action.[3] Consider, for example, value-orientations created by religious prophets. The core of every genuine prophecy, according to Weber, is 'an orientation to certain integral values', an orientation which bestows on the world a 'systematic and coherent meaning' and at the same time 'organize[s] practical behavior into a direction of life', resulting in a 'systematization of practical conduct' (E&S, pp. 450–1, 528). Weber's elucidation of the concept of 'personality', moreover, is strikingly similar to his account of religious prophecy. Personality, for Weber, is constituted by that which every prophecy demands: 'a constant and intrinsic relation to certain ultimate "values" and "meanings" of life, "values" and "meanings" which are forged into purposes and thereby translated into rational–teleological action' (R&K, p. 192). Without a value-orientation, it is impossible to have a genuine personality. Value-orientations, in short, are at once cognitive and conative: every value-orientation, religious or secular, involves an integration of meanings, values and dispositions and represents a practical 'stand in the face of the world' at the same time that it expresses a 'systematic and rationalized "image of the world" ' (FMW, p. 280).

Value-orientations interest Weber in two respects. In the first place, they are *causally* significant: they shape and guide human action. This does not mean that action is determined exclusively or even primarily by value-orientations. Value-orientations are complexes of ideas and dispositions, and Weber argues in a famous passage that 'interests (material and ideal), not ideas, directly govern men's conduct' (GAR, p. 252; FMW, p. 280). But while they do not directly determine behavior, value-orientations constitute the framework within which interests—especially ideal interests—are defined. In the terms of Weber's 'switchman' metaphor, value-orientations often determine 'the tracks along which action has been pushed by the dynamic of interest' (FMW, p. 280). That a full understanding of historical change is impossible without an understanding of the practical consequences of these value-orientations is a thesis that informs not only *The Protestant Ethic* but all of Weber's empirical work.

In the second place, value-orientations interest Weber because of their *moral* significance, because they lend coherence, dignity and meaning to human life. This theme, discussed in detail in Chapter 4, need only be adumbrated here. 'The dignity of the "personality" ', Weber writes, 'lies in the fact that . . . there exist values about which it organizes its life' (M, p. 55). It is because value-orientations are causally significant that they are morally significant: it is because they shape and guide action by giving a central direction to life—and thus distinguish human life from a mere 'event in nature' (M, p. 18)—that they are able to endow life with a coherent meaning and dignity. This intermingling of empirical and normative perspectives is responsible for the resonance of Weber's discussion of values and value conflict—but also for the ambiguity of some of his fomulations. The empirically indispensable but at the same time morally charged notions of value-orientation and value sphere again and again lead him into a 'gray zone'[4] between analysis and evaluation, where empirical claims and normative postulates are not easily disentangled.

Weber's conception of the clash of value-orientations rests on his account—part philosophical, part sociological—of the struggle for meaning in the modern world. New conceptions of the meaning of life—and thus new value-orientations—derive chiefly from charismatic figures (especially religious prophets) and from what Weber calls the 'natural rationalistic need of intellectualism to conceive the world as a meaningful cosmos' (E&S, p. 505). Thus in order to understand Weber's conception of the clash of value-orientations in modern society, we must first examine his account of the changing significance of charisma and intellectual need as sources of value-orientations in the modern rationalized world.

A charismatic figure is an individual who is believed to possess 'supernatural, superhuman, or at least specifically extraordinary [*ausseralltäglichen*] power or qualities' and who, as a result, is set apart from ordinary men and endowed with a special authority (W&G, p. 179; E&S, p. 241).[5] Charismatic authority, however, differs sharply from the authority of a sacred tradition or of a fixed and explicit set of rules: it is creative, disruptive, revolutionary. The charismatic leader 'preaches, creates, or demands *new* obligations'; he 'transforms all values and breaks all traditional and rational norms'; he radically alters the 'central attitudes and directions of action' of his followers. In short, he creates a new value-orientation and strives to impose it on others. Charisma is thus a powerful force of historical change; in premodern times, it is '*the* great revolutionary force'. Because charisma is essentially creative and disruptive, the emergence of charismatic leaders always sharpens the clash of value-orientations. For every charismatic figure creates and promotes a new value-orientation that inevitably collides with existing ones (E&S, pp. 243, 245, 1115).

A second source of novel value-orientations is the need, experienced most urgently by intellectuals, to perceive the world as a meaningful totality. The intellectual 'seeks in various ways, the casuistry of which extends into infinity, to endow his life with a pervasive meaning, and thus to find unity with himself, with his fellow men, and with the cosmos' (E&S, p. 506). The intellectual search for meaning, like the charismatic generation of new value-orientations, is essentially creative. The individual cannot discover the meaning of life through conceptual or empirical analysis; he must forge such meaning himself through a free act of the human spirit. And like charismatic value-creation, intellectual value-creation is divisive: new value-orientations created by intellectuals inevitably collide with existing ones.

Both charismatic and intellectual value-creation, then, contribute to value conflict. Not much more than this can be said about the clash of value-orientations from an ahistorical point of view. Weber's account of value conflict, however, is an *historical* one. The intellectual struggle for meaning and the charismatic creation of new value-orientations take place under very different conditions today than formerly. As political and economic rationalization progress, 'discipline inexorably takes over ever larger areas [, a development that] . . . more and more restricts the importance of charisma' (E&S, p. 1156).[6] Rationalization, moreover, limits the significance not only of charismatic value-creation but of all individual value-creation, indeed of all individual action: 'the waning of charisma generally indicates the diminishing importance of individual action' (E&S, pp. 1148–9). But if rationalization diminishes the *causal* significance of individual acts of value-creation, it does not diminish their *moral* significance. Individual value-creators lose their power to bind communities together: the 'prophetic *pneuma*, which in former times swept through the great communities like a firebrand, welding them together' (FMW, p. 155), does not have this power in the rationalized societies of today. But value-creation by individuals retains its significance as a great *divider* of communities. The struggle between ultimate value-orientations in the modern world is not, as formerly, a struggle of entire solidary communities against one another: it is increasingly a struggle of small sects, and ultimately a struggle of individuals (cf. FMW, p. 282).

Rationalization, far from rendering insignificant the clash of value-orientations, in fact sharpens this clash. At the same time that it weakens the binding force of charisma, it accentuates the urgency of the search for meaning by individuals:

> As intellectualism suppresses belief in magic, the world's processes become disenchanted, lose their magical significance, and henceforth simply 'are' and 'happen' but no longer signify anything. As a consequence, there is a growing demand that the world and the total pattern of life be subject to an order that is significant and meaningful. (E&S, p. 506)

Instead of abating, the need for meaning becomes more acute with the progress of rationalization, especially with the development of the scientific world-view and the attendant 'disenchantment' of the world. Yet at the same time that it becomes more acute, the need for meaning becomes more difficult to satisfy, for the scientific 'disenchantment' of the world carries with it the message of its own barrenness as a source of meaning. Science yields no value-orientations: individuals must create these themselves. And so long as each individual is impelled to create his own value-orientation, with no guidance from science, indeed with no objective guidance at all, value-orientations will continue to conflict.

It is the essential subjectivity of value-orientations that assures value conflict. Value-orientations are subjective in three distinct senses. First, they are *inner properties* of individuals—complexes of beliefs, attitudes, value commitments and dispositions. Thus Weber remarks that a charismatic shift in value-orientations involves a 'subjective or *internal* reorientation' (E&S, p. 245). Secondly, value-orientations are subjectively *generated*. They cannot be automatically imposed on individuals;[7] they must be created or actively embraced by individuals. The individual may—indeed must, if his life is to be a truly human one—choose his own 'fate': he must forge the 'meaning of [his] activity and existence' (M, p. 18).[8]

Finally, only a *subjective validity* can be claimed for value-orientations. As general conceptions of the nature of life and the world, as *Weltanschauungen*, value-orientations embody knowledge claims; but these claims have no objective validity. Scientific knowledge, for Weber, is objective: 'scientific truth is precisely what is *valid* for all who *seek* the truth' (M, p. 84). The 'knowledge' embodied in value-orientations, in contrast, is valid *not* for all who seek meaning and direction in life, but only for each individual. Objective scientific knowledge is radically distinct from the metaphysical knowledge embodied in subjective value-orientations: science yields no *Weltanschauungen*, and value-orientations can claim no support from science. 'We cannot learn the *meaning* of the world', Weber writes, 'from the results of its analysis, be it ever so perfect' (M, p. 57). Not only the knowledge claims but also, of course, the value commitments embodied in value-orientations have only a subjective validity. Science yields no value commitments (though it presupposes some; cf. FMW, p. 143), and it is impotent to arbitrate between conflicting value commitments. Weber is quite emphatic on this last point:

> Even such simple questions as the extent to which the end should sanction unavoidable means ... or how conflicts between several concretely conflicting ends are to arbitrated, are *entirely matters of choice or compromise*. There is no (rational or empirical) scientific procedure of any kind whatsoever which can provide us with a decision here. (M, pp. 18–19, emphasis added)

Value-orientations, then, are subjective in a triple sense: they are constituted by inner beliefs and dispositions, created out of inner need independently of external causes, and endowed with only a subjective validity.

This threefold subjectivity explains why conflict between value-orientations cannot be rationally resolved. But the mere existence of conflict implies nothing about its significance. The clash of value-orientations, for example, might be interpreted as analogous to the clash of interests in a pluralistic political system or the clash of preferences in a market economy—as 'manageable' if not exactly benign. Neither conflicting political interests nor conflicting economic preferences can be reconciled through any scientific procedure. According to theories of the pluralistic polity and the market economy, however, they can be 'harmonized' through the mediating institutions of representative government and the free market. Perhaps value conflict, like political and economic conflict as conceived by theorists of pluralism, would be managed, mediated, sublimated: transformed, in short, into regulated competition through some neutral institutional mechanism which itself would stand above all conflict. (Some such neutral mechanism through which conflicts among value-orientations could be mediated is implied in the phrase 'the marketplace of ideas'.) If this could be done, then the clash of value-orientations could be of limited significance. Individuals would continue to create divergent value-orientations, but these value differences could be easily accommodated: they would not threaten the social order.

Weber, however, derides the 'optimistic syncretism' (M, p. 57) that minimizes the seriousness of value conflict; his vision of the clash of value-orientations—informed, no doubt, by his acute awareness of the great social conflicts of his time[9]—is much darker than the one sketched above. For Weber, value-orientations are at the very core of the personality: they are serious, consequential, even fateful. The clash of value-orientations, since it can involve conflict over the most fundamental issues of social life, *can* threaten the cohesion and stability of the social order. There may be conflict, for example, over the legitimacy of the institutions of representative government—institutions that in the long run can only function to *mediate* conflict, as they are supposed to do in the pluralist world-view, to the extent that they are not the *objects* of conflict.

Because it may involve conflict over fundamental, all-embracing conceptions of the nature and meaning of life, then, the clash of value-orientations can indeed undermine social cohesion. Whether or not it will in fact do so at a particular time in a particular society cannot be determined *a priori*, for this depends on a number of empirical questions. First, what is the 'incidence' of value-orientations in the society? Not all individuals have value-orientations in Weber's strong sense of the term: not all individuals systematically organize their action into a 'direction of life' based on a core of consciously integrated values and meanings (although, according to Weber, such an integrated value-orientation is what distinguishes a truly human life from a mere 'event in nature'—see Chapter 4, Section 1).

Value conflict will be intensified or muted as more or fewer individuals create or adopt value-orientations.

Secondly, what is the degree of heterogeneity among value-orientations? There is a suggestion in Weber's work that heterogeneity tends to increase over time as widely shared religious world-views are eroded by the progress of science, leaving individuals to create value-orientations on their own, and as new provinces of activity—Weber mentions specifically the esthetic and erotic spheres—come to be conceived as universes of 'consciously grasped independent values which exist in their own right' (FMW, p. 342; see the following section). The greater the heterogeneity of value-orientations, the more intense will be the conflict among them.

Finally, what is the social and political content of value-orientations? To what extent do value-orientations call into question the legitimacy of the political order? To what extent does value conflict concern basic structural and institutional features of the social order? The more salient the social and political content of value-orientations, the greater will be the strain on social cohesion.

THE CLASH OF VALUE SPHERES

In 'Science as a Vocation', Weber writes that the 'value spheres of the world stand in irreconcilable conflict with each other' (FMW, p. 147). This claim differs sharply from his argument about the clash of value-orientations. The latter belongs to a well-defined philosophical tradition, that of ethical relativism and subjectivism (though Weber places more emphasis on comprehensive world-views and less on discrete value judgments than do most moral philosophers). The argument about value spheres, on the other hand, defies easy characterization or classification. Based on a quasi-philosophical, quasi-sociological analysis of the norms and values immanent in different 'life spheres',[10] it is a difficult and obscure argument, but one nevertheless central to Weber's vision of the world.

A value sphere, for Weber, is a distinct realm of activity which has its own inherent dignity, and in which certain values, norms, and obligations are immanent. Consider, for example, politics.

Whatever ends he pursues, the politician must be guided by an 'ethic of responsibility'. This is not a value-orientation, nor does it imply any particular value-orientation. The ethic of responsibility is consistent with the pursuit of any political ends and the use of any means. It governs not what a politician should do, but how he should decide what to do. The ethic of responsibility is not a world-view: it is a conception of the mode of decision-making appropriate to, indeed obligatory for, a politician. This ethic requires two things of the politician: that he 'give an account of the foreseeable results of [his] action' (FMW, p. 120); and that, in full awareness of the conflict between what is required of him as a politician and what may be required of him from the point of view of some other value sphere, he be prepared to use morally questionable and, if necessary, violent means to realize political ends, thus endangering 'the salvation of [his] soul' (FMW, p. 126). In so far as an individual does not meet these responsibilities, in Weber's view, he is not a true politician, though his conduct might be praiseworthy from the point of view of an extra-political value sphere.

The politician's obligation to act according to an ethic of responsibility, according to Weber, is an objective one, arising from the specific nature of political activity—from the fact that 'the attainment of "good" ends' may require the politician to use the specific and 'morally dubious' means available to him, namely 'power backed up by violence' (FMW, pp. 119, 121). In what sense, though, does an *obligation* arise from this fact (assuming, *arguendo*, that it is a fact)? Can this be consistently argued by the man who tirelessly advocates a sharp fact–value distinction? I think it can. In the first place, the ethic of responsibility does not commit the politician to any substantive values or ends. The requirement that the politician take into account the probable consequences of his action is a purely formal one. Moreover, even this is not a categorical but a hypothetical requirement. Weber readily admits that 'one cannot prescribe to anyone whether he *should* follow an ethic of conviction or an ethic of responsibility' (GPS, p. 546; FMW, p. 127). *If*, however, an individual wishes to be a political actor—i.e. to pursue ends with means that are backed ultimately by violence—and if he wishes actually to achieve his ends, whatever they may be, then he must not allow his action to be guided solely by the goodness of his intentions or the intrinsic rightness of his means. To do so would be to condemn his action to failure in a world in which good intentions are not guaranteed to produce good results. Instead, he must estimate the probable consequences of alternative courses of action and act in full awareness of these probable consequences. Only in this way can his political action have a chance of succeeding.[11]

Politics is 'inescapably bound to worldly conditions' (FMW, p. 339)—especially to the fact that the world is ethically irrational, a place of 'undeserved suffering, unpunished injustice, and hopeless stupidity'. In such a world, 'it is *not* true that good can follow only from good and evil only from evil, but . . . often the opposite is true' (FMW, pp. 122–3). Good intentions can fail to produce good results; irreproachable means can lead to disastrous consequences. The politician must therefore acknowledge the irreconcilable 'tension between means and ends'; he must take account of the 'average deficiencies of people'; he must not confuse ethics with efficacy; he must 'give an account of the foreseeable results of [his] action'; he must be willing, if need be, to 'pay the price of using morally dubious means or at least dangerous ones' that may have 'evil ramifications'; and he must assume the burden of deciding in concrete cases the extent to which an end '"justifies" the ethically dangerous means and ramifications' (FMW, pp. 120–1). These obligations are immanent in political activity in the sense that effective political action, whatever the ends to which it is oriented, presupposes their fulfillment.

The obligations of the politician, then, are not ethical obligations. The 'must' in 'the politician must act according to an ethic of responsibility' is not a specifically moral or ethical 'must'. It is rather a pragmatic 'must', based not on an ethical theory but on a theory of the conditions for successful political activity. Acting according to an ethic of responsibility, for Weber, is an indispensable means to all specifically political ends. Weber thus does not violate his fact–value distinction in deriving obligations from certain general 'facts' about political activity. These facts may be disputed, but the logic of the argument is unimpeachable.

Weber's account of politics illustrates three significant aspects of his conception of value spheres. First, value spheres, unlike value-orientations, are not created by individuals: they exist independently of and prior to the individuals who participate in them. Value spheres have an objective existence, based on the objective requirements of particular 'forms of life'. They may evolve over time as new forms of social life emerge; but the individual confronts them as given, as existing independently of his own action.

Secondly, there is no 'ultimate' value sphere from which to arbitrate between conflicting obligations immanent in different spheres. Consider, for example, the value spheres of politics and brotherly conduct. Immanent in the political sphere is an ethic that requires the individual to calculate the consequences of his action before acting; immanent in the value sphere of brotherly conduct, by contrast, is an ethic that requires the individual to act lovingly toward his neighbor, and ultimately even toward his enemy, regardless of the consequences (FMW, p. 330). The conflict between political rationality and brotherly love is irreconcilable: it cannot be resolved within any higher order value sphere, for no such higher order sphere exists. Every value sphere is a *particular* realm of activity in which particular norms are immanent. There are no universal value spheres—and hence no universal norms deriving from them. Torn between conflicting obligations deriving from different value spheres, the individual must simply choose: 'According to our ultimate standpoint, the one is the devil and the other the God, and the individual has to decide (*entscheiden*) which is the God *for him* and which is the devil' (GAW, p. 546; FMW, p. 148). Weber emphasizes the naked non-rationality of this choice. It cannot be guided by science; nor can it be determined by the norms of a higher value sphere, for choice is the task of life itself, not of any particular realm of life.

Thirdly, that the individual must choose which value sphere to serve does not imply that conflict between value spheres is subjective. Value-orientations are subjective, and conflict among them reflects the different ways in which individuals satisfy their need for meaning. But value spheres exist and conflict independently of the conflict of individual value-orientations. The clash between the political value sphere and the sphere of brother-liness, for example, is inherent in the respective inner logic of political and brotherly conduct; it is independent of any conflict that might exist between the value-orientations of particular politicians and those of individuals committed to an ethic of brotherly love. The clash of value-orientations is subjective in the sense that it arises out of the ever-shifting differences in individuals' fundamental beliefs and dispositions; the clash of value spheres, on the other hand, is objective in the sense that it arises out of differences in the inner structure and logic of different forms of social action.

Weber's understanding of the social world as composed of a plurality of value spheres, each with its own immanent and autonomous norms, is similar to the vision of society implicit in Hindu metaphysics and ethics:

> The Hindu order of life made each of the different occupations an object of a specific ethical code, a Dharma ... The caste order allowed for the possibility of fashioning the Dharma of each single caste, from those of the ascetics and Brahmins to those of the rogues and harlots, in accordance with the immanent and autonomous laws of their respective occu-pations. War and politics were also included ... This *specialization of ethics* allowed for the Indian ethic's quite unbroken treatment of politics by following politics' own laws. (FMW, p. 123, emphasis added)

But while the Indian vision conceives the various value spheres as harmoniously integrated into a rational social and cosmic order, Weber conceives them as locked in irreconcilable conflict with one another. There are two reasons for this sharp difference in perspective.

First, Weber's conception of the relation of the individual to the value spheres differs radically from the Indian conception. The individual, in the Hindu vision, never need choose between conflicting obligations arising from different value spheres. The obligations he must fulfill are unambiguously dictated by the caste position into which he is born. According to the doctrine of the transmigration of souls, however, the individual who fulfills the obligations of his caste will be reborn in a higher caste; the individual who does not will be reborn in a lower caste. An individual's caste position is thus merited, if not exactly chosen. Because the hierarchy of castes is clearly defined, so is the individual's long-term self-interest: to improve his caste position in subsequent incarnations. The individual is never torn by choice. He is born into a value sphere—into a distinct set of caste-based obligations—and it is in his own interest to fulfill these duties, and these alone, so as to assure his spiritual progress.

In Weber's conception, by contrast, the individual cannot escape the burden of choice. Because of the dissolution of ascriptive ties, he must forge his own relationship to the various value spheres. Because the spheres 'cross and interpenetrate' (M, p. 18), he must often choose between irreconcilable obligations. And because the spheres are not arranged into a universally recognized social and cosmic hierarchy, the individual can rely on no universally valid standard to guide his choice between conflicting demands. Though the value spheres have an objective existence, conflicts among them can be resolved, for any given individual, only through purely subjective choice.

Secondly, and more important, Weber postulates an intrinsic connection between the historical process of rationalization and the intensification of antagonisms among the value spheres. One aspect of rationalization is an increasing consciousness of what Weber calls the '*innere Eigengesetzlichkeiten der einzelnen Sphären*'—meaning an increasing awareness of the *causal, axiological, and normative autonomy* of the individual value spheres, or in other words an increasing awareness that conduct in each value sphere takes place according to its own laws, has its own inherent dignity or value, and generates its own norms and obligations. This growing consciousness of the autonomy of the various value spheres intensifies the tensions among them:

> The rationalization and the conscious sublimation of man's relations to the various spheres of values, external and internal, religious and worldly, have pressed towards making conscious the internal and lawful autonomy [*Eigengesetzlichkeit*] of the individual spheres, thereby letting them drift into those tensions which remain hidden to the original naive naturalness of man's relation to the external world. (GAR, p. 541; FMW, p. 328)

This dense and difficult passage announces the central theme of 'Religious Rejections of the World and their Directions' (FMW, pp. 323–59), Weber's final and most thorough discussion of value spheres: that rationalization in the religious, economic, political, esthetic, erotic, and intellectual realms engenders a growing consciousness of the autonomy of these spheres of value, thereby intensifying the 'antagonism of inner meanings' (*Sinnfeindschaft*) among them. Here I give a schematic account of Weber's (already highly schematic) discussion.

Rationalization is the leading theme of Weber's studies of religion, as of his empirical work as a whole.[12] Religion, according to Weber, arises out of magic and is originally indistinguishable from it: both magic and primitive religion are means of securing worldly goods—riches, health, long life, good harvests. As it is rationalized, however, religion comes to be conceived as an *autonomous* value sphere, explicitly distinguished from and opposed to magic and other worldly value spheres. Rationalization creates and progressively intensifies tensions between religious and 'worldly' values and obligations. In practice, of course, religion is continually forced to accommodate to worldly demands, to make concessions, for example, concerning economic, political, intellectual and sexual conduct. But despite these compromises, the principled and conscious antagonism between religious and worldly values that emerges as religion is rationalized has decisively shaped the consciousness—and the conscience—of modern man.

The religious 'rejection of the world' emerges not from rationalization as such—for many different and even contradictory religious developments are in some sense rationalizations—but from the distinctive pattern of rationalization associated with religions carried by prophets promising salvation from earthly distress.[13] This pattern of rationalization has four salient features. First, the hope for salvation is displaced from this world (*Diesseits*) to a world to come (*Jenseits*). As this happens, 'worldly' obligations and activities are devalued:

life in this world comes to be regarded as a merely provisional form of existence . . . action in this world becomes oriented to one's fate in the world beyond ... [and] the problem of the basic relationship of god to the world and its imperfections presses into the foreground of thought. (W&G, p. 407; E&S, p. 521)

Secondly, a systematically unified world view develops:

> To the prophet, both the life of man and the world, both social and cosmic events, have a certain systematic and coherent meaning, to which man's conduct must be oriented if it is to bring salvation and after which it must be patterned in an integrally meaningful manner. (E&S, p. 450)

The conflict between this 'conception of the world as a meaningful totality' and the apparent irrationality and meaninglessness of much of empirical reality, between the world as it ought to be and as it actually is, 'produces the strongest tensions in man's inner life as well as in his external relationship to the world' (E&S, p. 451).

Thirdly, rationalization involves the systematic unification of religious ethics. The 'complex of heterogeneous prescriptions and prohibitions' (E&S, p. 437) that make up a religious ethic in its early stages gives way to a single requirement: that the individual maintain the permanent disposition (*Dauerhabitus*) necessary and sufficient to assure his salvation (or to assure one who believes in predestination—a Calvinist, for example—*of* his salvation). Every genuine religious prophet promotes an ethical systematization of this kind by commanding that an individual's total way of life (*Lebensführung*) be oriented to the pursuit of a single sacred value (*Heilsgut*) rather than to the pursuit of various worldly goods (*weltliche Guter*) (GAR, pp. 540–1; FMW, pp. 327–8).

Finally, rationalization involves what Weber calls the 'sublimation of piety' (E&S, p. 438). By sublimation Weber means the increasing concern of religious ethics with the inner state (*Gesinnung*) of the individual and the decreasing concern with the external course of action. To the extent that such a 'sublimation' occurs, the particular actions of an individual are not scrutinized separately for their conformity to discrete ritual or ethical prescriptions but are instead treated as 'symptoms and expressions of an underlying ethical total personality' (*ethischen Gesamtper-sönlichkeit*): individual conduct is judged not by the correctness of external actions but by the 'value of the total personality pattern' (E&S, pp. 533–4).

This rationalization of religious ethics reveals an irreconcilable tension inherent in the concept of rationality. The rationality demanded by 'sublimated' religious ethics places the ethical value of an act solely in the actor's inner disposition (*Gesinnung*) and not at all in the act's consequences (*Folgen*); the actor is not ethically responsible for the consequences of his action, but must simply maintain the proper *Gesinnung* and leave the consequences to God (M, p. 16; FMW, p. 339). The religious demand that one act in this *wertrational* or value-rational manner (see Chapter 2, pp. 51–2) is wholly incommensurable with the pragmatic requirement, immanent in all 'worldly' action, that one act in a *zweckrational* or instrumentally rational manner. *Wertrational* action strives for inner purity, guided by a conscious belief in the intrinsic value (*Eigenwert*) of a certain inner state, whatever its consequences; *zweckrational* action strives for external success, guided by a conscious weighing of ends, means, and unintended but foreseeable secondary consequences.

The opposition between *Wertrationalität* and *Zweckrationalität* finds concrete expression in the antagonism between the religious ethic of brotherliness and the objective necessity for *zweckrational* conduct in the economic and political spheres. Rational action in these spheres, if it is to stand any chance of 'succeeding', i.e. of achieving the desired results, whatever these may be, is 'inescapably bound to worldly conditions, conditions which are remote from brotherliness' (GAR, p. 552; FMW, p. 339). Rational economic conduct, for example, is inextricably bound up with market struggles, which, in their consummate impersonality, are the epitome of unbrotherliness. Calculation is 'required' in the sense that whoever scorns it must face 'economic failure and, in the long run, economic ruin' (E&S, p. 585). Purely *zweckrational* behavior is not optional: it is 'prescribed by objective situations . . . under penalty of economic extinction' (W&G, p. 900; E&S, p. 1186). Yet the 'absolute depersonalization' of this calculating attitude is 'contrary to all the elementary forms of human relationships' and is 'fundamentally alien' to the religious ethic of brotherliness (E&S, pp. 636–7). Similarly, rational political action has its own 'objective pragmatism', follows its own 'external and internal laws'. The more it is rationalized in terms of its own autonomous laws—'the more matter of fact and calculating politics is, and the freer of passionate feelings, of wrath, and of love it becomes'—the more politics is estranged from the demands of the religious ethic of brotherliness (FMW, pp. 334–5).

In practice, of course, religious ethics have always had to make compromises with the demands of economic and political life. But despite these compromises, the tension between the religious and the economic and political value spheres has steadily intensified as a result of *diverging processes of rationalization*: the substantive rationalization of religious ethics in the direction of a *Gesinnungsethik* and pure *Wertrationalität*, and the formal rationalization of economic and political action in the direction of increasing calculability and pure *Zweckrationalität*.

Tension among value spheres is complicated and intensified by the rationalization and conscious cultivation of esthetic and erotic enjoyment, which develops in reaction to the formal rationalization of economic and political action and in competition with the substantive rationalization of religious ethics. As the world is increasingly intellectualized and rationalized, art and eros, because of their 'essentially non-rational or anti-rational character', receive an ever-stronger value accent (*Wertakzent*) as life-enhancing antidotes to the deadening dominance of *zweck-rational* action and intellectual culture. Art and eros emerge as autonomous value spheres, as realms of 'ever-more consciously grasped independent values'. The more these values are con-sciously elevated to the level of absolute values, and the more they are conceived as harboring the 'most real kernel of life' (*realsten Lebenskern*), the more esthetic and erotic enjoyment take over 'the function of a this-worldly *salvation* from the routines of everyday life and, above all, from the increasing pressures of theoretical and practical rationalism' (GAR, pp. 554–5; FMW, pp. 341–2, 345). This attempt to escape the anesthetizing influence of economic, political and intellectual rationalization, however, is in one sense doomed to failure, for the accentuation and conscious cultivation of esthetic and erotic values is itself a *form* of intellectualizing rationalization. Weber hints at this self-defeating result—another instance of the paradox of unintended consequences—when he writes that

> the spheres of the irrational, the only spheres that intellectualism has not yet touched, are now raised into consciousness and put under its lens. This modern intellectualist form of romantic irrationalism ... may well bring about the very opposite of its intended goal. (GAW, p. 540; FMW, p. 143)

As a method—even if ultimately self-defeating—of achieving a *this-worldly* salvation from 'mechanisms of rationalization' (FMW, p. 345), the conscious cultivation of esthetic and erotic enjoyment collides with religion and its promise of an *other-worldly* salvation. It is true that some esthetic and erotic experiences may have a psychological and even a physiological affinity with certain religious experiences (FMW, pp. 342–3, 347–9), but this affinity only intensifies their 'antagonism of inner meanings' (*Sinnfeindschaft*) (FMW, p. 348).[14]

Consider finally the intellectual value sphere. The intellectual realm emerges as an autonomous value sphere in ancient Greece with the development of self-consciousness about concepts:

> In Greece, for the first time, appeared a handy means by which one could put the logical screws upon somebody so that he could not come out without admitting either that he knew nothing or that this and nothing else was the truth, the *eternal* truth that never would vanish ... That was the tremendous experience which dawned upon the disciples of Socrates. And from this it seemed to follow that if one only found the right concept of the beautiful, the good, or, for instance, of bravery, of the soul, ... that then one could also grasp its true being. And this, in turn, seemed to open the way for knowing and for teaching how to act rightly in life and, above all, how to act as a citizen of the state; for this question was everything to the Hellenic man, whose thinking was political throughout. (FMW, p. 141)

Through this 'realization of the significance of the concept'

(FMW, p. 141), the intellectual realm emerges as not only an autonomous but also an imperialistic value sphere, claiming to show men 'the "way to true being", the "way to true art", the "way to true nature", the "way to true God", the "way to true happiness" ' (FMW, p. 143)—claiming, in short, for conceptual analysis the power to make all of human life conform to reason.

The rise of modern science at once enhances and diminishes the autonomy of intellect and its power to shape conduct. Modern science 'disenchants' the world by construing it as a rationally calculable and manipulable causal mechanism (FMW, p. 350). On the one hand, the theoretical understanding of the disenchanted world as a causal mechanism subject to no 'mysterious incalculable forces' makes possible its practical manipulation. It is intellect that rules the disenchanted world, a world in which 'one can, in principle, master all things by calculation' (*alle Dinge durch ... Berechnen beherrschen*) (FMW, p. 139). Disenchantment in this sense dramatically enhances the power of intellect. On the other hand, disenchantment divests the world not only of 'mysterious incalculable forces'—i.e. of obstacles to instrumentally rational action—but also of its *meaning*. For to the extent that science conceives the world as a causal mechanism operating in accordance with wholly non-ethical laws, it 'develops refutations of every intellectual approach which in any way asks for a "meaning" of worldly occurrences' (GAR, p. 564; FMW, p. 351). The cosmos of natural causality postulated by science cannot be reconciled with the cosmos of ethical meaning required by religion—and, more generally, by intellect. Disenchantment in this respect diminishes the autonomy of intellect by withdrawing the imprimatur of scientific legitimacy from intellect's prime ambition: to show the 'way to true being' by discovering the meaning of the world and guiding conduct in accordance with this meaning.

Disenchantment radically transforms the intellectual value sphere. If 'we cannot learn the meaning of the world from the results of its analysis' (M, p. 57)—the lesson of disenchantment—then the *value* of intellectual activity becomes problematic.[15] For Socrates and his followers, the value of intellectual activity was profoundly social: conceptual analysis could show men 'how to act rightly in life and, above all, how to act as a citizen of the state' (FMW, p. 141). For modern man, however, the value of intellectual activity is essentially individual: intellect cannot guide the life of a society; it can only enrich the lives of individuals. No longer a means of discovering true being and guiding right conduct, intellectual activity comes to be pursued as an end in itself. Intellectual (and, more broadly, cultural) values are increasingly understood as values to be appropriated by individuals striving for a worldly self-perfection (*innerweltlichen Selbstvervollkommung*). The pursuit of these 'highest worldly goods', like the pursuit of esthetic or erotic values, assumes the function of providing a this-worldly salvation—a salvation through self-perfection from the routines of workaday existence in a world denuded of its meaning (GAR, pp. 568–9; FMW, pp. 354–6). But this worldly striving for 'salvation' through the creation or appropriation of intellectual and cultural values is entangled in a web of tensions. As a quest for salvation *through* rational intellectual activity, it collides with the search for salvation *from* rationalization and intellectualism through the pursuit of esthetic and especially erotic enjoyment. As a striving for salvation through an accumulation of *worldly* values, it collides with the religious quest for an *otherworldly* salvation. And as a form of *self*-cultivation, it creates an 'unbrotherly aristocracy that is independent of all personal ethical qualities of man' (GAR, p. 569; FMW, p. 355) and thus collides with the value sphere of *brotherly* conduct.[16]

Apart from these tensions with other value spheres, the striving for salvation from meaninglessness through intellectual cultivation is condemned to fail even in its own terms:

The peasant, like Abraham, could die 'satiated with life'. The feudal landlord and the warrior hero could do likewise. For both fulfilled a cycle of their existence beyond which they did not reach ... But the 'cultivated' man who strives for self-perfection, in the sense of acquiring or creating 'cultural values', cannot do this. He can become 'weary of life' but he cannot become 'satiated with life' in the sense of completing a cycle. For the perfectibility of a man of culture in principle progresses indefinitely, as do the cultural values. And the segment which the individual and passive recipient or the active co-builder can comprise in the course of a finite life becomes

the more trifling the more differentiated and multiplied the
cultural values and the goals for self-perfection become. Hence
the harnessing of man into this external and internal cosmos of
culture can offer the less likelihood that an individual would
absorb either culture as a whole or what in any case is 'essential'
in culture. Moreover there exists no definitive criterion for
judging the latter. It thus becomes less and less likely that
'culture' and the striving for culture can have any inner-worldly
meaning for the individual. (FMW, p. 356)

Self-perfection through intellectual cultivation thus not only
collides with the demands of other value spheres: it is also
impossible in principle. It is with this bleak assessment of the
meaning of intellectual culture that Weber concludes his discussion of the irreconcilable antagonisms among the main value
spheres of the modern world.

VALUE CONFLICT AND WEBER'S DIAGNOSIS OF MODERNITY

'Religious Rejections of the World and their Directions' (FMW,
pp. 323–59) is widely recognized as a key text, as the final
expression of Weber's 'diagnosis of modernity and its problems of
meaning' (Schluchter, 1979, p. 64). The heart of this diagnosis is
the claim that 'the various value spheres of the world stand in
irreconcilable conflict with each other' (FMW, p. 147). But what
is the status of this diagnosis? Is it a *metaphysical* diagnosis, an
expression of Weber's personal world-view, his personal value-
orientation? Or is it an *empirical* diagnosis, a scientific account of
value conflict in the modern world?

Weber's tantalizing introduction to 'Religious Rejections'
suggests that his theory of the clash of value spheres is neither a
metaphysical nor an empirical diagnosis of modernity but merely
an ideal-typical conceptual scheme. Not metaphysical: Weber
insists that his schematic analysis of value spheres 'does not teach
a philosophy of its own'. Nor empirical: he admits that the
'individual spheres of value are prepared with a rational consistency which is rarely found in reality'. The value spheres are not
actually existing phenomena but 'theoretically constructed
[ideal] types of conflicting "life orders"', and the conflicts among

them are not actual but possible conflicts: they are conflicts that would occur *if* 'certain rational conclusions, which can be established theoretically, [were] drawn in reality', *if* rules of conduct were deduced with perfect consistency from divergent ultimate values. Like all ideal-typical constructions, the ideal-typical presentation of value spheres makes it possible to 'determine the degree of approximation of the historical phenomenon to the theoretically constructed type'. To this extent, as Weber readily concedes, the ideal-typical construction of value spheres is 'merely a technical aid which facilitates a more lucid arrangement and terminology' (FMW, pp. 323–4).

Is Weber's theory of the clash of value spheres, then, not a theory at all, but merely a heuristic device? Is the burgeoning literature on Weber's diagnosis of the plight of man in modern society much ado about nothing? Certainly the tone of much of this literature, especially that which focuses narrowly on the *Angst*-ridden perorations to Weber's speeches on politics and science as vocations, is unduly portentous. But Weber's ideal-typical construction of conflicting value spheres is more than a mere technical aid. Though it is not an empirical account of actually existing value conflict, it is an account of *real tendencies* toward irreconcilable value conflict—tendencies inherent in the dynamic of rationalization that has shaped and that continues to shape the modern world. For rationlization leads to a growing consciousness of the autonomy (*Eigengesetzlichkeit*) of the individual value spheres, thus creating *latent tensions* among them which may develop—under conditions Weber does not specify—into overt conflicts.

The meaning of *Eigengesetzlichkeit*, however, is far from clear, mainly because Weber does not distinguish the causal, axiological, and normative dimensions of the concept from one another. A value sphere may be 'autonomous' in three distinct senses: conduct within that sphere may take place according to its own laws (causal autonomy), may have its own inherent dignity or intrinsic value (axiological autonomy), or may generate its own norms and obligations (normative autonomy). The three senses are logically independent of one another. Thus, for example, causal autonomy does not entail axiological autonomy. The fact that conduct within the economic sphere follows distinctively economic laws—laws based on the functioning of markets—does not bestow a special dignity or intrinsic value on economic conduct. Nor does causal autonomy entail normative autonomy, except in a very restricted sense. The fact that economic action follows laws of its own does mean, in a certain sense, that the economic actor 'must' obey certain specifically economic norms—norms requiring him to act according to calculations of economic advantage. If he fails to obey these norms, he risks economic ruin. Prudent self-interest, then, 'requires' him to obey these norms. But he is under no *obligation* to obey them—no obligation, that is, arising from any *value* other than mere self-interest. Only when a value sphere generates obligations not reducible to self-interest does it have normative autonomy in a strong sense.

The economic sphere, in short, is autonomous in the causal sense—to the extent that economic action does in fact follow laws of its own—but not in the axiological or the normative sense. Not *necessarily*, that is. For the norms of economic action *might* be experienced as binding obligations. Thus for the ascetic Puritan entrepreneurs of early modern capitalism, the pursuit of wealth was a sacred obligation, an obligation wholly independent of, indeed fundamentally inimical to, rational eudaemonistic self-interest.[17] Whether or not a sphere of action is autonomous in the normative or axiological sense, then, depends on how the activity is *experienced* by participating individuals, which in turn depends on their fundamental beliefs and value commitments, i.e. on their *value-orientations*. Economic activity was experienced as axiologically and normatively autonomous by Puritan ascetic entrepreneurs, but it is not experienced in this way by hedonists. Similarly, the intellectual sphere was experienced as autonomous in these senses by Socrates and his disciples, but not by the Sophists, for whom intellectual activity was a *means* to extra-intellectual ends. Axiological and normative autonomy, in short, are *subjective* properties, dependent on and relative to the experience of particular individuals, as shaped by their beliefs and value commitments. Causal autonomy, on the other hand, is an *objective* property. The extent to which a given sphere of activity follows laws of its own can, in principle, be objectively determined, however difficult this may be in practice.

If Weber's conception of autonomy (*Eigengesetzlichkeit*) is ambiguous, his conception of value spheres is equally ambiguous. His use of the single term 'value sphere' to include the economic and political spheres on the one hand and the religious, intellectual, cultural, esthetic, and erotic spheres on the other obscures crucial differences between the two groups. The former are autonomous in the causal sense, the latter in the axiological and normative sense. The former emerge as autonomous spheres through processes of objectification, the latter through processes of internalization and conscious cultivation. The autonomy of the former is objective and self-perpetuating, that of the latter subjective and dependent on continually renewed value commitments of individuals. The norms of the former constrain conduct 'from without' (cf. E&S, p. 1116), requiring an individual to act in a purely *zweckrational* (instrumentally rational) fashion so as to be successful in his pursuit of economic or political ends; the norms of the latter constrain conduct 'from within', requiring an individual to act in a purely *wertrational* (value-rational) fashion so as to be consistent in his pursuit of ultimate values.[18]

'Value sphere', then, used in reference to the economic and political realms, is misleading, for these objectified institutional orders leave no room for the systematic subjective orientation of conduct to some consciously upheld ultimate value—yet such an orientation is precisely what constitutes the religious, intellectual, cultural, esthetic, and erotic realms as autonomous value spheres.

More importantly, Weber's use of the term 'value sphere' to include the economic and political realms as well as the religious, intellectual, cultural, esthetic, and erotic spheres obscures his analysis of the tensions inherent in the modern social world. It implies that these are primarily tensions among conflicting ultimate values. This, however, is not the case. More significant than tensions among ultimate values, in Weber's diagnosis of modernity, are tensions between ultimate value commitments on the one hand and the requirements of successful economic and political action, requirements that are alien to *all* questions of ultimate value, on the other. In the technical idiom of *Economy and Society*, it is not conflict between different forms of *wertrational* action that Weber emphasizes in his diagnosis, but conflict between the purely *zweckrational* action required in the economic and political realms and the *wertrational* action demanded by every commitment to ultimate values. Conflict among values is overshadowed by conflict over the meaning of rationality—over whether rationality is or should be divorced from ultimate values, as are formal rationality and purely *zweckrational* action, or whether rationality is essentially linked to ultimate values, as are substantive rationality and purely *wertrational* action.

The 'world dominion of unbrotherliness' that Weber emphasizes at the end of 'Religious Rejections of the World' results not from irreconcilable conflict among ultimate values but from the impossibility of living up to the norms of brotherly conduct in a society dominated by formally rational economic, administrative and political structures:

> in the midst of a culture that is rationally organized for a vocational workaday life, there is hardly any room for the cultivation of acosmic brotherliness, unless it is among strata who are economically carefree. Under the technical and social conditions of a rational culture, an imitation of the life of Buddha, Jesus, or Francis seems condemned to failure for purely external reasons. (FMW, p. 357)

Impersonal calculating conduct, which requires the individual to treat others as means to his own ends, is objectively necessary in the economic and political spheres; brotherly conduct, as a result, can flourish only in the *interstices* of the modern social order.[19] This severe restriction of the scope and significance of brotherly conduct results not from a tension between conflicting ultimate values, between conflicting standards of substantive rationality, but rather from the impotence of demands for substantive rationality in a society dominated by objectified economic and political structures that perpetuate themselves according to an inexorable logic of purely formal rationality, a logic that excludes all considerations of substantive rationality, all questions of ultimate value. Weber's casual use of 'value sphere', in short, together with his shorthand pronouncements to the effect that the 'gods' and values of the various social spheres are locked in an 'irreconcilable death-struggle' (M, p. 17), obscures rather than clarifies his diagnosis of modernity.

The tensions inherent in the modern social order, then, are not primarily tensions among conflicting ultimate values. Still, tensions between formal and substantive rationality, between *Zweck-* and *Wertrationalität*, between value-drained worldly tasks and the pursuit of ultimate values *mean the same thing for the individual* as tensions between conflicting standards of substantive rationality, between conflicting maxims of *Wertrationalität*, between conflicting ultimate values. Both types of tensions—the former deriving from the special nature of modern economic and political structures, the latter from an increasing awareness of the incommensurability of ultimate value standpoints—force the individual who wishes to consciously guide his life to *choose* between competing definitions of rationality. Whether it is a choice between formal and substantive rationality or between conflicting standards of substantive rationality, between *Zweck-* and *Wertrationalität* or between conflicting maxims of *Wertrationalität*, this choice cannot itself be a rational one, for it is precisely criteria of rationality that must be chosen. Modern man, then, cannot escape making a criterionless and therefore non-rational choice about the very meaning of rationality. Weber's diagnosis of modernity, of what it means to live in a pervasively rationalized world, thus calls into question the very notion of leading a rational life. How can man live rationally if the very meaning of rationality is something that must be freely and arbitrarily chosen? It is these dilemmas that I explore in my final chapter.

NOTES TO CHAPTER 3

1 Schluchter (1981) relates Weber's theory of value conflict to what he calls Weber's 'development history'. Bruun (1972, esp. pp. 178–99) analyzes Weber's conception of value conflict in relation to his methodological views. Perhaps the most penetrating criticism of Weber's conception of value conflict is that of Strauss (1953, pp. 64–78).

2 The exact term 'value-orientation' is not Weber's. But since the notion, variously expressed, of an 'orientation to certain integral values' (*Orientierung an einheitlichen Werten*) (E&S, p. 528) that guides conduct and gives meaning to the world is developed by Weber in his discussions of both prophecy and personality, it seems reasonable to designate this concept with the more economical expression 'value-orientation'.

3 Weber employs two distinct though related conceptions of meaning. On the one hand, meaning is that aspect of every concrete action that makes the

action *intelligible* to the actor himself, to fellow actors and to observers. That action is meaningful in this sense is a presupposition of sociology—at least of the interpretive (*verstehende*) sociology advocated by Weber. On the other hand, Weber is concerned not only with the meaning of concrete individual actions but also with 'ultimate meaning', with the meaning of life as a whole. Meaning in this sense is an integrated complex of beliefs and dispositions that imposes coherence and direction on the chaos of immediate experience. That an individual's life be meaningful in this sense, according to Weber, is a presupposition of a truly human (as opposed to a merely natural) existence (see Chapter 4, Section 1). A value-orientation endows an individual's life with meaning in this second, broader sense.

4 I am indebted to Robert K. Merton for this formulation.

5 See Camic (1980) for a closely reasoned discussion of the 'varieties, preconditions, and consequences' of charisma—a discussion that begins with a critical examination of Weber's use of the concept.

6 Recent history, to be sure, calls into question Weber's emphasis on the decreasing causal significance of charisma in rationalized societies. See, for example, Neumann (1944, pp. 83ff.) for a discussion of the charismatic foundation of the German National Socialist state.

7 The development of 'brainwashing' techniques in cults and prisoner-of-war camps suggests that, under some circumstances, value-orientations *can* be imposed on individuals. For Weber, though, an imposed value-orientation would not be a 'genuine' one. This points up the unresolved tension between empirical and normative elements in Weber's conception of value-orientations.

8 Here, of course, Weber diverges from Marx—or at any rate from 'vulgar Marxism'—in insisting that value-orientations, though often displaying a marked affinity with class interests, are not mere epiphenomena of them (M, p. 56). Despite his explanation of many religious ideas—and of course secular ideologies as well—in terms of the class-based need to legitimate one's good (or ill) fortune (cf. FMW, pp. 270–7), Weber holds that conflict between *Weltanschauungen* is independent of conflict between class interests. Class interests determine the range of value-orientations that may most comfortably and conveniently satisfy the 'metaphysical need for a meaningful cosmos' (FMW, p. 281); they may determine, in other words, the path of least resistance. But they do not unequivocally determine value-orientations: these are freely created or freely adopted by individuals. Indeed, experience shows that individuals of the same class—especially intellectuals—*can* create or subscribe to radically different world-views and that these world-views can shape their practical activities in radically different ways. A corollary of Weber's anti-Marxian view that value-orientations are subjectively generated, of course, is that value conflict would persist even if class conflict were eliminated.

9 Mitzman (1971, p. 3) stresses this theme: 'At the heart of Weber's vision lies only the truth of his epoch, his country and his station, the truth of a bourgeois scholar in Imperial Germany'.

10 'Life spheres' and 'value spheres' are here used interchangeably. The ambiguity in the notion of value sphere is examined in pp. 82–7.

11 This does not mean that a politician must take into account *nothing but* probable consequences. Faced with a situation in which the attainment of a good end requires the use of ethically dubious means (e.g. deception or violence), the politician must choose between the importance of the end and

the gravity of the contemplated violation of ethical norms. As a politician, he strives to eliminate ethics from political reasoning (FMW, p. 334); but as a man he acknowledges the authority of the ethical norms that he may have to violate. Confronting such a choice between achieving an important political end and adhering to an ethical norm, the politician 'somewhere . . . reaches the point where [following Luther] he says: "Here I stand; I can do no other" '. The dignity and pathos of politics lies in the politician's assumption of the heavy responsibility for such a choice, which no rules can guide: to assume this responsibility, in Weber's view, 'is something genuinely human and moving' (FMW, p. 127).

12 Though concerned primarily with the *economic* consequences of religious rationalization—with the way in which different paths of rationalization promote or hinder the development of capitalism—Weber also explores its *moral* and *psychological* consequences. I discussed the former in Chapter 1, pp. 22–9; here I am concerned with the latter.

13 'Prophets and priests', Weber writes, 'are the twin bearers of the systematization and rationalization of religious ethics' (E&S, p. 439). However, they tend to rationalize religious ethics in different directions. (See Schluchter, 1979 and 1981, for a systematic analysis of the different paths of religious rationalization distinguished by Weber.) Prophecy produces 'a centralization of ethics under the aegis of religious salvation' (E&S, p. 438) and attempts to organize life through an *inner* ethical systematization (*gesinnungsethische Systematisierung*) (GAR, p. 367). Priests, on the other hand, bring about through preaching and pastoral care the 'routinization of prophetic demands into specific prescriptions'. Casuistically elaborated, these specific prescriptions are in one sense 'more rational' than the prophetic ethic. But at the same time, they lack the inner unity (*inneren Einheit*) that the prophet introduces into ethics. Priests are more concerned with the 'external appearance of a single act', prophets with the 'meaningful significance [of each act] for the total relationship to the god' (E&S, p. 465). The ethical rationalization carried by prophets intensifies tensions between religion and worldly value spheres; that carried by priests reduces these tensions by legitimizing compromises between religious and worldly obligations. Here I give an ideal-typical account of the way in which the ethical rationalization promoted by prophets intensifies tensions between religious demands and worldly activities: I ignore the factors that tend to mitigate these tensions.

14 Rational religious ethics must reject the esthetic sphere, to the extent that the latter claims to provide a 'this-worldly, irrational salvation', as a 'realm of irresponsible indulgence and secret lovelessness . . . To the creative artist, however, as well as to the esthetically excited receptive mind, the ethical norm as such may easily appear as a coercion of their genuine creativeness and innermost selves' (GAR, pp. 555–6; FMW, p. 342). And here is Weber on the 'antagonism of inner meanings' between religion and sexual love: 'The euphoria of the happy lover . . . always meets with the cool mockery of the genuinely religiously founded and radical ethic of brotherliness . . . In the eyes of this ethic, the most sublimated [i.e. consciously cultivated] eroticism is the counterpole of all religiously oriented brotherliness, in these aspects: it must necessarily be exclusive in its inner core; it must be subjective in the highest imaginable sense; and it must be absolutely incommunicable'. The lover, however, 'realizes himself to be rooted in the kernel of the truly living, which is eternally inaccessible to any rational endeavour', religious or secular (GAR, pp. 561–2; FMW, pp. 347–9).

15 Weber grapples with this problem in 'Science as a Vocation' (FMW, pp. 139–56) and in 'Religious Rejections of the World and their Directions' (FMW, pp. 350–7). Arthur Mitzman (1971, p. 219) has aptly remarked that these essays contain 'Weber's most troubled reflections on the problems of meaninglessness in modern society'.

16 Weber notes that 'the barriers of education and of esthetic cultivation (*Bildungs- und Geschmackskultur-Schranken*) are the most intimate and the most insuperable of all status differences' (FMW, p. 354).

17 For Weber's remarks on the peculiar irrationality, from the standpoint of self-interest, of the Puritan entrepreneur's attitude toward wealth, see PE, pp. 53, 70, 78.

18 This contrast, to be sure, is overdrawn. The intellectual value sphere, for example, does not fit neatly into the second category. For in so far as the 'objective world' constrains individual scientists 'from without', requiring them to act in a *zweckrational* fashion in order to establish successful knowledge claims, science is formally similar to politics and economics. (I am indebted to Robert K. Merton for this observation.)

19 Not only brotherly conduct, oriented to the ultimate value of *caritas*, but all conduct oriented to ultimate values can flourish only in the interstices of the formally rational social and economic order. This seems to be what Weber is suggesting at the end of 'Science as a Vocation':

> Precisely the ultimate and most sublime values have retreated from public life either into the transcendental realm of mystic life or into the brotherliness of direct and personal human relations. It is not accidental that our greatest art is intimate and not monumental, nor is it accidental that today only within the smallest and most intimate circles, in personal human situations, in *pianissimo*, that something is pulsating that corresponds to the prophetic *pneuma*, which in former times swept through the great communities like a firebrand, welding them together. (GAW, p. 554; FMW, p. 155)

4

Weber's Moral Vision

Weber presents himself as an empirical scientist, not as a moral philosopher. It is true that he has no moral philosophy in the traditional sense. He elaborates no rules of individual conduct, harbors no vision of an ideal society. And the standard terms of moral argument—good, right, ought, should—are conspicuously absent from his vocabulary. Yet the whole of his scientific work is informed by a fundamentally moral impulse—by a passionate concern with the 'fate of man' in contemporary capitalist civilization (Löwith, 1982, p. 20).[1] This concern is embodied in Weber's empirical interpretation of modernity in terms of its 'specific and peculiar rationalism' and in his moral response to this rationalized world. The former I have explored in the preceding chapters; the latter—the set of ideas and ideals comprising Weber's moral response to modernity—I explore in this chapter.

Weber's moral thought is highly idiosyncratic, and it invites criticism in a number of respects.[2] In this chapter, however, my aim is neither to criticize nor to defend Weber's views but simply to reconstruct them from his very sketchy remarks on the subject and to present them in a clear and systematic manner. I focus on his conception of the nature and limits of moral rationality, and on his view of the relation between the freedom and moral rationality of the individual and the supra-individual rationality of the modern social order.

THE ETHIC OF PERSONALITY: FROM PHILOSOPHICAL ANTHROPOLOGY TO MORAL PHILOSOPHY

Weber's fact–value distinction is perhaps his best known contribution to moral philosophy. Echoing Hume, who was the first to question the legitimacy of deriving 'ought' from 'is', Weber insists on the absolute logical heterogeneity of empirical propositions and normative judgments (M, pp. 51, 58; R&K p. 274). This distinction, however, is more likely to obscure than to clarify the status of Weber's own moral ideals. For these *ideals* are derived from certain *ideas* about the nature of man—ideas that are at once empirical and normative. These ideas make up Weber's philosophical anthropology, his conception of the essence of human being, of what it is that distinguishes human life from other natural processes.[3]

At the heart of Weber's philosophical anthropology is the concept of meaning. Meaning is the essential property of human action; it is what distinguishes human actions from other natural events. Not all human behavior is meaningful, but conduct that is not meaningful is not specifically human; such conduct has more in common with non-human natural events than with meaningful action.

Meaning is intrinsically linked with rationality. Although Weber does not attempt to define 'meaning', he does delimit the domain of meaningful action through two kinds of examples: paradigmatic cases and borderline cases. Paradigmatic of unambiguously meaningful action are the two types of rational action: means–ends rational (*zweckrational*) and value-rational (*wertrational*) action. These have in common a self-consciousness on the part of the actor about his action: in both cases the actor knows what he is doing and does it deliberately. *Zweckrational* action is guided by the actor's conscious weighing of his ends, the various possible means to these ends, and the probable secondary consequences of employing these means. Similarly, *wertrational* action is marked by the 'clearly self-conscious formulation of the ultimate values governing the action and the consistently planned orientation of its detailed course to these values' (E&S, p. 25). Paradigmatically, then, meaningful action is action that is rational in the sense of deliberately planned and consciously guided.

The outer limits of meaningful action are marked by two borderline cases: traditional and affectual behavior. In contrast to the two types of rational action, these have in common the actor's relative lack of conscious awareness of and deliberate control over his conduct. The degree of awareness and control—and thus the degree of 'meaningfulness' of traditional and affectual behavior—varies from case to case. On the one hand, strictly traditional behavior is 'very often a matter of almost automatic reaction to habitual stimuli'. Similarly, purely affectual behavior may take the form of an 'uncontrolled reaction to some exceptional stimulus' (E&S, p. 25). In these cases, conduct passes from the domain of meaningful action—and thereby from the domain of truly human action—to the realm of merely reactive behavior. On the other hand, an actor may deliberately and self-consciously persist in traditional patterns of action, or he may deliberately decide to release consciously experienced emotional tension in a certain way. In these cases conduct is no longer purely traditional or purely affectual: it has an important rational component and is therefore meaningful.

Action is meaningful, then, in so far as it is rational, meaning consciously guided. Freedom, too, is intrinsically linked with rationality:

> We associate the highest measure of an empirical 'feeling of freedom' with those actions which we are conscious of performing rationally—i.e., in the absence of physical and psychic 'coercion,' emotional 'affects' and 'accidental' disturbances of the clarity of judgment, in which we pursue a clearly perceived end by 'means' which are the most adequate in accordance with the extent of our knowledge. (M, pp. 124–5)

Rational action, then, is at the same time free and meaningful action. Together, these qualities distinguish human actions from other events in nature. *Truly human action is rational, free and meaningful; natural events are non-rational, unfree and devoid of meaning*.

Not all human conduct, of course, is rational, free and meaningful; much, indeed most human behavior falls below the threshold of the truly human. Thus consciously meaningful action is only a 'marginal case': 'In the great majority of cases actual action goes on in a state of inarticulate half-consciousness or actual unconsciousness of its subjective meaning' (E&S, p. 21). Some human conduct—the behavior of the insane, for example—shares fully the non-rationality, unfreedom and meaninglessness of natural events; most falls somewhere in between the poles of the truly human and the merely natural. Weber's conception of *truly* human action is thus not a conception of *typically* human action: it is a polar concept, an ideal-typical limiting case.

Weber's conception of the truly human applies not only to individual actions but also to human life as a whole. Just as it is meaning that distinguishes a truly human individual action from an event in nature, so it is meaning that distinguishes a truly human life from a chain of natural events. A human life, like an individual action, is meaningful in so far as it is consciously guided, i.e. in so far as it is rational, in the broadest sense of this term. And just as a consciously guided individual action is a free action, so too a consciously guided life—and only such a life—can be considered free.

Meaning, rationality and freedom, however, have a different significance in reference to a human life as a whole than they do in reference to a single action. Morally neutral when applied to a single action, they become morally charged when applied to life as a whole. Thus for an individual action to be meaningful, it is sufficient that it be consciously oriented to some purpose, however insignificant. Swatting a fly is every bit as meaningful, in itself, as rescuing children from a burning building. A meaningful action can just as well be morally indifferent or even blameworthy as morally praiseworthy. A meaningful life, in contrast, is one endowed with *dignity* and thereby, in Weber's view, with moral worth. Meaning and moral dignity derive from the systematic integration of individual actions into a unified life pattern based on certain fundamental values. A life that lacks this systematic unity is not a meaningful life, even if it is composed of a string of meaningful actions.

Rationality, too, is a concept that is morally neutral on the level of individual action but morally charged on the level of life as a whole. While the rationality of an individual action may depend solely on the appropriateness of the means to a single given end, whatever its value and whatever its relation to other ends, the rationality of a life as a whole depends on the coherence of an individual's ends and values, the constancy over time with which he pursues these ends and values, and the clarity of his self-understanding. The rationality of an individual action, in short, may be no more than a matter of efficiency; the rationality of a complete life, on the other hand, is always a matter of *integrity*.

Freedom, finally, has a deeper and richer meaning when applied to life as a whole than it does when applied to an individual action. For a single action to be free, it is sufficient that it be uncoerced by physical or psychic factors beyond the agent's conscious control. Life as a whole, in contrast, has the potential to be free not in the merely negative sense of being uncoerced, but in the positive sense of being *autonomous*, i.e. guided by norms of the individual's own making.

Weber's philosophical anthropology is summed up in his conception of *personality*. (Personality, for Weber, is not a psychological but a philosophical concept.) The qualities that distinguish a truly human action from an event in nature—meaning, rationality and freedom—converge in this conception:

> The freer the action . . . i.e. the less it has the character of a natural event, the more the concept of personality comes into play. The essence of personality lies in the constancy of its inner relation to certain ultimate values and life-meanings, which, in the course of action, turn into purposes and are thus translated into teleologically rational action. (GAW, p. 132; R&K, p. 192)

Here Weber presents personality as a methodological ideal type. Only in so far as individuals have personalities can science genuinely understand individuals and their actions. Natural events, however regular, can never be 'understood', in Weber's special sense of this term, for they have no intrinsic meaning. They can be explained by being subsumed under general laws, but they cannot be understood in terms of their meaning. To the extent that human lives remain natural events, they too can be explained but not understood. But to the extent that individuals become personalities, their lives cease to be mere events in nature; they become consciously guided, meaningful, and therefore understandable. Personality, then, is what distinguishes the truly human and the merely natural from the point of view of science: the truly human personality and his actions are understandable; the 'natural' man and his conduct are not.

But personality is also what distinguishes the truly human and the merely natural from the point of view of moral philosophy: personality is a moral ideal as well as a methodological ideal type. Weber regards as '*objectively* valuable [his emphasis] those innermost elements of the "personality", those highest and most ultimate value judgments which determine our conduct and give meaning and significance to our life' (M, p. 55). The morally charged qualities that distinguish a truly human life from an event in nature—dignity, integrity and autonomy—are inherent in the concept of personality. Thus Weber emphasizes the 'dignity of the "personality" ', which 'lies in the fact that for it there exist values about which it organizes its life' (M, p. 55). Integrity, too, is bound up with the idea of personality, for personality is constituted by the '*constancy* of its inner relation to certain ultimate values and life-meanings' (GAW, p. 132; R&K, p. 192, emphasis added). Autonomy, finally, derives from the individual's deliberate shaping of his own personality through his choice of the ultimate values and meanings that are to structure his life-activity.

Personality, however, is a purely formal moral ideal. To become a personality, an individual must be committed to certain fundamental values, but he need not be committed to any particular values. Any value or complex of values to which the individual can consciously and consistently orient his existence is as good as any other. More broadly, Weber's philosophical anthropology and moral philosophy as a whole are purely formal. Every truly human life, according to Weber, has the same form: it is oriented to some central value or complex of values. Weber affirms this *form* as a central moral ideal: every person, in his view, *should* orient his life to some central value. But while the form of the truly human life is fixed, the content varies widely: the central values to which life can be oriented range from purely personal values 'within the sphere of the person's "individuality" ' (M, p. 55) to suprapersonal intellectual, cultural, moral, religious, social or political values. And within any one of these domains—within the political domain, for example—there is a plurality of irreconcilably opposed ultimate value positions to which an individual can orient his life. Weber's philosophical anthropology is silent about what the content of the truly human life is, and his moral philosophy is silent about what this content should be.[4]

Despite its formal character, Weber's ethic of personality imposes arduous demands on individuals. To be a personality, one must systematically unify the whole of one's existence. To consistently observe certain standards in one's external conduct is not enough: one's ultimate value-orientation, whatever its substantive content, must inform inner bearing as well as external conduct. Such thoroughgoing unity does not come naturally: it can be achieved (or rather approached: to be a personality is not a goal that one can achieve once and for all, but an ideal that one can at best approximate) only through a continuous and strenuous conscious effort. For only through vigilant awareness and active exertion can the individual progress from a 'natural' to a 'truly human' state, from a life governed by the chaotic impulses of his raw, unformed, given nature to one governed by the coherent values and meanings of his consciously formed personality.

In the rigor of its demands, Weber's ethic of personality is a heroic ethic, an aristocratic ethic, an ethic of virtuosi—to use terms he himself employs. Weber distinguishes explicitly between 'heroic' and 'average' ethics, for example, in a letter criticizing a pseudo-Freudian attempt to construe mental health as a moral ideal:

> All systems of ethics, no matter what their substantive content, can be divided into two main groups. There is the 'heroic' ethic, which imposes on men demands of principle to which they are generally *not* able to do justice, except at the high points of their lives, but which serve as signposts pointing the way for man's endless *striving*. Or there is the 'ethic of the mean', which is content to accept man's everyday 'nature' as setting a maximum for the demands which can be made. (S Tr, pp. 385–6)

A heroic ethic may well start from a 'pessimistic assessment of the "nature" of the average man' (S Tr, p. 386). Unlike the ethic of the mean, however, it is not content to accept this average nature as normatively valid, as setting a limit to the ethical demands that can 'reasonably' be made. Instead, it imposes on men arduous demands that can be realized only by the select few and only 'at the high points of their lives'. In this sense, Weber's is clearly a heroic ethic.

A radical bifurcation of humanity is implicit in this aristocratic moral philosophy. The mass of men are condemned to the meaninglessness of a merely natural existence; only the ethical virtuosi are privileged to lead a truly human existence. No special dignity inheres in human nature as such. As Walter Kaufmann (1967, p. 512) has written about Nietzsche's moral philosophy, to which Weber's bears a striking resemblance:[5]

> such dignity is not *gegeben* but *aufgegeben*, not a fact but a goal that few approach ... to raise ourselves above the senseless flux, we must cease being merely human, all-too-human. We must be hard against ourselves and overcome ourselves; we must become creators instead of remaining mere creatures.

In Weber's as well as Nietzsche's moral vision, few succeed in becoming creators of their personalities, in bestowing meaning and dignity on their lives; most remain mere creatures, mired in the meaningless flux of the merely natural. And for the latter, in Weber's as in Nietzsche's moral universe, there is no redemption.

THE LIMITS OF MORAL RATIONALITY

There is a disturbing paradox at the heart of Weber's moral philosophy. The truly human life is one that is guided by reason. To live a life informed by reason, an individual must become a personality. To become a personality, he must commit himself to certain fundamental values. But this commitment, though it is the foundation of every personality, and thus of every rational life, cannot itself be guided by reason, for in Weber's view there is no rational way of deciding among the plurality of conflicting possible value commitments. Every rational life, in short, is founded on a non-rational choice.[6]

This paradox arises from the disjunction between the *anthropological* perspective on reason that informs the normative strand of Weber's moral philosophy and the *logical* perspective on reason that informs his metaethical views.[7] Anthropologically understood, reason is a distinctively human power of conscious self-formation. Through the exercise of reason, an individual can transform unconscious impulses and semiconscious habits into conscious purposes, integrate these purposes into a systematic life plan, and in this way consciously shape and create a personality out of the tangle of contradictory impulses that comprise raw, unformed human nature. This broad anthropological understanding of reason underlies Weber's normative ethic. Grounded in a conception of the distinction between rational man and irrational nature (including raw human nature), this ethic bids men become personalities and thereby realize their true humanity through the exercise of reason. It is by virtue of his unwavering commitment to reason in this anthropological sense that Weber can be understood as an advocate of the values of the Enlightenment and, in particular, as a defender of moral rationality.[8]

Conjoined with Weber's essentially anthropological ethic of self-realization through reason, however, is a metaethical theory emphasizing the narrowly limited moral significance of reason. The perspective that informs this metaethical theory is that of logic, not philosophical anthropology; reason is conceived narrowly as a power of determining empirical truths and making logical deductions, not broadly as a self-formative power. Reason in this restricted sense can resolve moral disagreements that are based on factual disagreements, and it can criticize inconsistencies in moral argument. Fully rational and conclusive moral argument, however, is impossible in principle. To be sure, actions can be justified in terms of value judgments, and particular value judgments in terms of more general ones. But every such chain of reasoning eventually reaches some ultimate value judgment or value-orientation that cannot be rationally (i.e. empirically or logically) justified. There is an irreducible plurality of conflicting ultimate values, and among these the individual must simply choose.[9]

Both Weber's normative ethic and his metaethical theory emphasize the central moral significance of choice. But while the one conceives choice as a conscious, deliberate, commitment-founding, personality-forming and in these respects rational event, the other conceives choice as unguided by criteria and therefore non-rational. It is thus because rationality has both a broad anthropological sense and a narrow logical meaning in Weber's thought that a rational (in the anthropological sense) and therefore truly human life can be held to depend on a non-rational (in the logical sense) and therefore arbitrary choice.

In its emphasis on the moral significance of choice, Weber's moral thought displays a marked affinity with that of existentialism. This affinity is comprised by a shared conception of man as a self-creating being, a shared emphasis on the limits of moral rationality, and a shared conception of autonomy as a central moral ideal.

For existentialist thinkers, as for Weber, man makes himself, forms his own nature, creates his own personality through his choices. The central doctrine of existentialism, according to Alisdair Macintyre (1967, p. 149), is that 'men do not have fixed natures that limit or determine their choices, but rather it is their choices that bring whatever nature they have into being'. Similarly, Weber claims that 'life as a whole, if it is not to be permitted to run on as an event in nature but is instead to be consciously guided, is a series of ultimate decisions through which the soul ... chooses its own fate, i.e. the meaning of its activity and existence' (M, p. 18).

A second theme common to Weber and existentialist thinkers is that the most fundamental choices are necessarily non-rational. For while rational choice—choice governed by criteria—is possible, there are various conflicting criteria of rationality. These criteria must themselves be chosen, and *this* choice cannot be a rational one (cf. Macintyre, 1967, p. 149).[10]

The final and most crucial similarity between the moral thought of Weber and that of existentialist thinkers is their overriding concern with autonomy.[11] In Kant's classic formulation, autonomy is the condition of being subject only to self-created and self-imposed obligations; heteronomy, in contrast, is the condition of being subject to obligations that one has not created. This morally charged opposition between autonomy and heteronomy persists in the moral thought of Weber and the existentialists, but the connection established by Kant between autonomy and rationality is severed. For Kant, autonomy resides in the rule-making of the 'rational will'—a will that can adopt as its own ruling principles only maxims that can be universalized. Universality is a necessary and sufficient condition of the rationality—and thus the rightness—of a moral principle; autonomous moral legislation is thus purely rational, having nothing to do with arbitrariness or choice (Olafson, 1967, pp. 39–40). For Weber and the existentialists, in contrast (and for Nietzsche, whose ideas deeply influenced their work), autonomy resides not in the formulation of universal laws but in the value-creating activity of a will unconstrained by any criteria— except, in Weber's case, by the criterion of self-consistency. Autonomous moral legislation depends on criterionless choice.

MORAL CHOICE IN THE MODERN WORLD

Despite his proto-existentialist emphasis on criterionless choice, Weber remains committed to moral rationality as an ideal—and not only to reason in the anthropological sense but to the moral significance of logical and scientific rationality. This commitment to moral rationality is manifest in his conception of the role of science in what might be called moral education (though Weber does not use this expression): a strictly rational enterprise that helps individuals 'gain clarity' about their choices (FMW, p. 151; Levine, 1981b). For Weber as well as for existentialist thinkers, ultimate choices are necessarily non-rational, for they cannot be guided by any objective criteria (since choice-guiding criteria must themselves be chosen). But for Weber there is none the less an element of rationality in choice. For while fundamental choices cannot be rationally governed, they can be rationally *framed*. Choice situations, that is, can be rationally analyzed, and the logical implications and empirical consequences of the various possible choices can be specified. Choice occurs, in short, between rationally delineable alternatives. It is this rational analysis of choice situations that is in Weber's view the task of moral education, for it permits individuals to gain clarity about their choices, and thus to choose in full awareness of what they are embracing and of what they are forgoing.

Moral education employs both empirical and philosophical analysis to help individuals gain clarity about their choices. Empirical analysis, to begin with, can call attention to what Weber calls 'inconvenient facts'—facts that do not fit individuals' party opinions or personal world-views. To make students acknowledge such facts is in Weber's view 'the primary task of a useful teacher'; it is not a 'mere intellectual task' but a genuine 'moral achievement' (FMW, p. 147). More generally, empirical analysis can help individuals gain clarity about particular socio-ethical problems by specifying the probable consequences— especially those that are unintended but none the less scientifically foreseeable—of alternative courses of action. Such analysis often reveals that some ends can be achieved only with morally dubious means, or that the realization of a desired end entails undesirable secondary consequences. When this is the case, moral education can confront the individual with the necessity of choosing between the end and the unavoidable means, or between the end and the undesired secondary consequences (M, p. 23). But while the teacher, as moral educator, can help the individual to recognize *that* he must choose, he cannot help the individual to determine *how* he must choose: moral education, as Weber conceives it, is strictly formal.

While empirical analysis helps individuals gain clarity about their evaluative response to particular problems of social life, philosophical analysis helps them gain clarity about their value-orientations—about the meaning and structure of their lives as a whole. Philosophical analysis does this by forcing individuals to consider the relations between their evaluative stands on particular socio-ethical issues and the 'ultimate *weltanschauliche* position[s]' from which such particular evaluations can be consistently derived:

> we [teachers] can and should state: In terms of its meaning, such and such a practical stand can be derived with inner consistency, and hence integrity, from this or that ultimate *weltanschauliche* position. Perhaps it can only be derived from one such fundamental position, or maybe from several, but it cannot be derived from these or those other positions. Figuratively speaking, you serve this god and you offend the other god when you decide to adhere to this position . . . Thus we can

... force the individual, or at least we can help him, to give himself an *account of the ultimate meaning of his own conduct* ... [A] teacher who succeeds in this ... stands in the service of 'moral' forces; he fulfills the duty of bringing about clarity and a sense of responsibility. (GAW, p. 550; FMW, pp. 151–2)

Clarity and responsibility are intrinsically linked; together they are a precondition of genuine moral autonomy. For only responsible ultimate value choices, only those made in full awareness of their logical implications, have moral dignity and contribute to moral development; all other choices are simply arbitrary acts, incapable of furthering the development of autonomous moral personality.[12]

Moral education is not confined to the classroom: it embraces all activities that help individuals gain clarity about the choices they face. Thus Weber's interpretation of modern society in terms of its peculiar rationality falls within the province of moral education, for it elucidates what is in Weber's view the fundamental moral problem of modernity: the problem of how individuals can preserve their true humanity—their autonomy, dignity and integrity—in the modern rationalized world.

From the point of view of the basic moral task of individuals— to develop autonomous personalities—the pervasive rationalization of social life poses a triple threat. First, the scientific disenchantment of the world makes more arduous the task of defining the meaning of life—a task that is a precondition for becoming a personality. For with the development of the scientific view of the world as a structure of causal relationships, it becomes increasingly difficult to conceive of the world as having an objective meaning. As a result, it is less and less likely that the individual will be able to derive the meaning of his life from any generally accepted conception of the meaning of the world as a whole. Instead, the individual is thrown back on his own resources. Starting from scratch, each individual must create anew the meaning of his own life. The task of forging on one's own an integral life-meaning is an arduous one, and one to which many individuals fail to measure up, allowing their lives instead 'to run on as an event in nature' (M, p. 18).

Secondly, the rationalization of the modern economic and

political order endangers human freedom.[13] Though modern capitalism is dependent on formally free labor, it is the locus of a powerful though impersonal form of coercion, employing as a sanction the 'loss or decrease of economic power and, under certain conditions . . . the very loss of one's economic existence':

> The private enterprise system transforms into objects of 'labor market transactions' even those personal and authoritarian-hierarchical relations which actually exist in the capitalistic enterprise. While the authoritarian relationships are thus drained of all normal sentimental content, authoritarian constraint not only continues but, at least under certain circumstances, even increases. The more comprehensive the realm of structures whose existence depends in a specific way on 'discipline'—that of capitalist commercial establishments—the more relentlessly can authoritarian constraint be exercised within them, and the smaller will be the circle of those in whose hands the power to use this type of constraint is concentrated and who also hold the power to have such authority guaranteed to them by the legal order. (E&S, p. 731)

An even more serious threat to freedom, according to Weber, is posed by the apparently inexorable extension of bureaucratic control over social life (Mommsen, 1974). Characterizing bureaucracy as 'that animated machine . . . busy fabricating the shell of bondage which men will perhaps be forced to inhabit some day, as powerless as the fellahs of ancient Egypt', Weber asks: 'How can one possibly save *any remnants* of "individualist" freedom?' (E&S, pp. 1402–3).

The final—and most insidious—threat posed by the process of rationalization to the development of autonomous moral personality derives from the increasing predominance of the instrumentally rational (*zweckrational*) orientation of action (Mommsen, 1974). While the ever-widening reach of the formally rational mechanisms of capitalism and bureaucracy threatens to curtail individual freedom from without, the steady diffusion of the *zweckrational* orientation threatens to subvert individual autonomy from within. This idea is not explicitly developed by Weber, but it is implicit in the structure of his moral thought.

The threat to individual autonomy posed by the increasing salience of *Zweckrationalität* is not readily apparent. *Zweckrationalität* appears to maximize individual freedom: the individual with a purely *zweckrational* orientation is by definition unhampered by the constraints of tradition, strong emotion, or ultimate value commitments. Yet this individual is free only in a purely negative sense. Consider two individuals. One is the embodiment of pure *Zweckrationalität*.[14] He is committed to no ultimate values and carried away by no violent emotions; he observes no customs, follows no habits, and abides by no rules—except, of course, the rules of marginal utility. He does nothing without a conscious decision, and every decision involves a similar calculation. He takes stock of his wants, orders them according to urgency, calculates the cost of satisfying them, predicts the secondary repercussions of pursuing them, and weighs costs against benefits—all without reference to ultimate values. The second individual, in contrast, does not simply consult his 'given subjective wants' (E&S, p. 26) in order to decide how to act. Instead, he derives his ends from his value commitments. He possesses a personality—a concept, it will be recalled, that 'entails a constant and intrinsic relation to certain "values" and "meanings" of life, "values" and "meanings" which are forged into purposes and thereby translated into rational-teleological action' (R&K, p. 192). This individual consciously strives to shape his life in accordance with his chosen ultimate value commitments.

Which individual is freer? The first individual, to be sure, is not bound, as is the second, by any ultimate value commitments, and is thus completely unfettered in his decisions. But in a deeper sense the first individual is less free. For he does not really choose his ends; his agenda of ends is in fact determined by his given subjective wants—by his 'raw' nature rather than by his consciously formed personality. In Kant's language, the first individual, far from being free, is at the beck and call of inclination: 'reason merely supplies a practical rule [in this case, the principles of marginal utility] for meeting the need of inclination' (1964, p. 81n). *Given* wants guide the first individual in his selection of ends; *chosen* ultimate values guide the second. Only the second individual is autonomous in Weber's sense. For autonomy does not connote the radical 'freedom from inner bonds' (*inneren Ungebundenheit*; W&G, p. 22) that characterizes pure *Zweckrationalität*, but rather the capacity of an individual to create his own moral personality by committing himself to certain ultimate values and meanings and organizing his life around them. Pure *Zweckrationalität*, in short, is morally dangerous because it is incompatible with genuine autonomy.

Faced with this threefold threat to the development of autonomous moral personality, the individual must make a fundamental choice. On the one hand, he may decide to reject the modern rationalized world. Thus, for example, instead of struggling on his own to create a meaning for his life, he may consciously and deliberately make the necessary 'sacrifice of the intellect' and 'return to the old churches, whose arms are opened widely and compassionately for him' (GAW, p. 554; FMW, p. 155). Instead of working to defend individual freedom *within* the modern rationalized politico–economic order, he may seek freedom *from* this rationalized world (Löwith, 1982, p. 52) and strive to realize his fundamental values in the interstices of the modern social order, in those spheres of social life, such as the 'brotherliness of direct and personal human relations' (FMW, p. 155), that have remained relatively untouched by the dynamic of rationalization. Or instead of trying to combine a commitment to ultimate values with the rational calculation of consequences involved in the *zweckrational* orientation of action, he may reject *Zweckrationalität* completely in favor of pure *Wertrationalität* (value-rationality) and orient his action to the realization of some absolute value or unconditional demand, paying no heed to the probable consequences of his action.

On the other hand, the individual may accept—indeed affirm—the modern rationalized world as the arena in which he will strive to become a personality. This is what Weber himself chooses to do, though he acknowledges the dignity of the conscious, deliberate, internally consistent decision to reject this world and argues that such a decision cannot be rationally criticized. Aware that the modern world harbors grave moral dangers, Weber sees it as offering at the same time a unique moral opportunity—the opportunity to achieve the special kind of dignity he associates with the 'ethic of responsibility'

(Schluchter, 1979). This dignity attaches above all to the politician who, forced to consider the use of morally dubious means to realize important ends, is 'aware of a responsibility for the consequences of his conduct and really feels such responsibility with heart and soul' (FMW, p. 127; cf. Chapter 3, pp. 70–1 above). But the ethic of responsibility is not a specifically political ethic; it is rather an extremely general ethical orientation applicable to many domains of social life.

Weber defines the ethic of responsibility in opposition to the ethic of conviction (*Gesinnungsethik*). They differ decisively with respect to what Weber calls the 'very first question' of ethics (FMW, p. 339):

(a) whether the intrinsic value [*Eigenwert*] of ethical conduct—the 'pure will' or the 'conscience' [*Gesinnung*] as it used to be called—is sufficient for its justification, following the maxim of the Christian moralists: 'The Christian acts rightly and leaves the consequences of his action to God'; or (b) whether the responsibility for the foreseeable—as possible or probable—consequences of the action is to be taken into consideration . . . Both [points of view] invoke ethical maxims. But these maxims are in eternal conflict—a conflict which cannot be resolved by means of ethics alone. (GAW, p. 467; M, p. 16; cf. FMW, pp. 120–8, 339)

The believer in an ethic of conviction, who takes the former attitude, considers the foreseeable consequences of his action ethically irrelevant; the believer in an ethic of responsibility, who takes the latter attitude, considers them ethically relevant in the highest degree, and feels personally responsible for them. The conflict between these two ethical orientations, Weber argues, 'cannot be resolved by means of ethics alone'. Each individual must resolve it for himself through an extra-ethical choice.

The choice between an ethic of conviction and an ethic of responsibility is ultimately a choice between two modes of rationality. Here again we encounter the central paradox of Weber's moral philosophy: in order to live a rational (meaning consciously guided) life, an individual must make a criterionless and in this sense non-rational choice between two irreconcilably opposed modes of rationality. To choose to be guided by an ethic of conviction is to adopt a purely *wertrational* (value-rational) orientation: it is to act, according to Weber's definition of *Wertrationalität*, which could serve equally well as a definition of the ethic of conviction, on the basis of a 'conscious belief in the unconditional, intrinsic value (*Eigenwert*) of some ethical, esthetic, religious or other form of behavior as such, independently of its consequences' (W&G, p. 17; E&S, pp. 24–5). Adopting an ethic of conviction thus entails the unreserved rejection, as ethically barren, of all rational reckoning of means and ends, all calculating of consequences—the rejection, in short, of the central elements of rational purposeful (*zweckrational*) action. To choose to be guided by an ethic of responsibility, on the other hand, is to commit oneself to precisely these central elements of *Zweckrationalität*. It is to reason in terms of means and ends; to 'give an account of the foreseeable results of one's action' (FMW, p. 120); to 'rationally weigh not only means against ends but ends against secondary consequences and finally also the various possible ends against one another', as Weber puts it in his definition of *Zweckrationalität* (W&G, p. 18; E&S, p. 26).

Yet the ethic of responsibility is *not* identical with pure *Zweckrationalität*. For pure *Zweckrationalität*, as I argued above, precludes any reference to ultimate value commitments: ends are determined by the urgency of an individual's 'given subjective wants' and by the ease of satisfying them, not by their 'worth' from the point of view of a system of ultimate values. The ethic of responsibility, on the other hand, is not merely compatible with a commitment to ultimate values, but demands just such a commitment. For responsibility is empty unless it is responsibility to some 'substantive purpose' (FMW, p. 116), unless it is informed by 'passionate devotion to a "cause" ' (FMW, p. 115).

Far from being identical with pure *Zweckrationalität*, the ethic of responsibility can best be understood as an attempt by Weber to integrate *Wertrationalität* and *Zweckrationalität*, the passionate commitment to ultimate values with the dispassionate analysis of alternative means of pursuing them. Thus Weber argues that the politician must weld 'warm passion' to a 'cool sense of proportion'—must combine passionate devotion to a cause with the 'ability to let realities work upon him with inner concentration and calmness' (FMW, p. 115). Put somewhat differently, the ethic of responsibility is an attempt by Weber to integrate reason in the anthropological sense with scientific rationality. Reason in the anthropological sense, it will be recalled (see pp. 98–100 above), is the distinctively human power to give meaning and dignity to one's life by adhering to a central value-orientation; while scientific rationality, as it relates to action, is the power to act on the basis of empirical knowledge of the causal relations linking ends, means and secondary consequences. The ethic of responsibility requires on the one hand that the development of personality through the exercise of reason in the anthropological sense be disciplined by the cool skepticism of scientific rationality so as to maximize the chances of actually realizing the values to which one is committed. It requires, in short, that ends determined in a *wertrational* manner be pursued with means selected in a *zweckrational* manner. On the other hand, the ethic of responsibility requires that scientific rationality serve reason in the anthropological sense, that the calculating attitude of *Zweckrationalität* be subordinated to the pursuit of ends chosen in a *wertrational* manner. For scientific rationality alone affords no basis for the conduct of life; in and of itself, like pure *Zweckrationalität*, it is ethically barren. Only by integrating the *wertrational* and *zweckrational* orientations, by joining reason in the anthropological sense to scientific rationality, can an individual live a truly human life *within* the modern rationalized world.

WEBER'S MORAL TEMPERAMENT

To choose between an ethic of conviction and an ethic of responsibility, then, is to choose between two modes of rationality: between pure *Wertrationalität* and a synthesis of *Wert-* and *Zweckrationalität*. The choice cannot itself be a rational one, for it is precisely the criteria of rationality that must be chosen. Weber's own allegiance to the ethic of responsibility—and thus to a synthesis of *Wert-* and *Zweck-rationalität*—reflects his deeply ambivalent attitude toward the processes of rationalization that have shaped and that continue to shape modern Western culture. Weber recognizes that the modern social world harbors grave moral dangers—dangers that arise directly from its specific and peculiar rationality. The 'tremendous cosmos of the modern economic order', based on the purely formal rationality of the market, 'determine[s] the lives of all the individuals who are born into this mechanism, not only those directly concerned with economic acquisition, with irresistible force' (PE, p. 181). Bureaucracy, because of its unsurpassable technical rationality the 'only really inescapable power', threatens to develop a stranglehold over all of social life, condemning man to 'social impotence' (E&S, p. 1403). Modern science, construing the world as a causal mechanism, has eroded older conceptions of the world as a meaningful cosmos and thereby saddled individuals with the arduous task of creating meaning for the world on their own. And the permeation of *Zweckrationalität* into all domains of social life threatens to take place 'at the expense of any commitment to ultimate values' (W&G, p. 22; E&S, p. 30), thus 'ethically neutralizing' the world (Schluchter, 1981, p. 51). In view of these serious threats to the development of autonomous moral personality—threats that are inherent in the modern rationalized social world—Weber acknowledges the dignity of those who deliberately reject this world in order to lead their lives outside the domain of the rationalized institutional orders.

Yet while he recognizes the legitimacy of a stance of uncompromising rejection of the modern world, Weber is himself committed to a radically this-worldly moral perspective: committed, that is, to struggling to lead a truly human life within the modern rationalized world. Like the Puritan ascetic, whom he so movingly portrays in his studies of religion, Weber too 'affirms individual rational activity within the institutional framework [*Ordnungen*] of the world, affirming it to be his responsibility as well as his means for securing certification of his state of grace' (E&S, p. 548).[15] More precisely, he affirms the ethical significance of rational action 'within the institutions of the world but in opposition to them' (E&S, p. 542). This ethos of engaged opposition, of responsible struggle, is crystallized in his attitude toward bureaucracy. Appalled by 'the idea that the world should be filled with nothing but those cogs who cling to a little post and strive for a somewhat greater one', Weber does not ask how it is possible to escape from the bureaucratized realms of life. Instead, he identifies the 'central question' as 'what we have to *set against* this [bureaucratic] machinery, in order to preserve a remnant of humanity from this parcelling-out of the soul, from this exclusive rule of bureaucratic life ideals' (quoted in Mitzman, 1971, p. 178).

The moral life, for Weber, is framed by a series of tensions: between ultimate values and recalcitrant reality, between warm passion and a cool sense of proportion, between ends and means, between *Wertrationalität* and *Zweckrationalität*, between reason in the anthropological sense and scientific rationality, between idealistic striving and realistic adaptation to the possible—between, in sum, the ethically rationalized personality, committed to certain standards of *substantive* rationality, and the ethically neutral social world, governed by mechanisms of purely *formal* rationality. These tensions can be definitively resolved in two ways: by abandoning one's ideals, one's ultimate value commitments, and learning to adjust or adapt to the world as it is (and to oneself as one happens to be) in a purely *zweckrational* manner; or by denying the significance of what Benjamin Nelson (1971, p. 162) has called the 'social reality principle', by rejecting a concern with the consequences of one's action and striving to realize one's values in a purely *wertrational* manner. Weber rejects the first way of resolving the tensions on principled grounds as incompatible with the core requirement of a truly human life—that the individual give his life a coherent meaning and direction by committing himself to certain ultimate values and orienting his action to their realization; he rejects the second way of resolving them on personal grounds as indicative of an inability to 'bear the fate of the times like a man' (FMW, p. 155). For Weber himself, or for any individual committed to struggling to realize ultimate values within the modern rationalized world, the tensions can never be resolved: they constitute the enduring framework within which all moral conduct takes place (cf. Schluchter, 1979, p. 53).

What Raymond Aron (1971, p. 93) has called a 'metaphysics of struggle', part Darwinian, part Nietzschean, lies at the foundation of Weber's thought. Weber repeatedly emphasizes the inevitability of conflict—among nations, among classes, among individuals, and, not least, within each individual. Moreover, he affirms the value—the 'productivity', in Löwith's expression (1982, p. 57)—of conflict and contradiction. 'The highest ideals', for Weber, are 'formed only in the struggle with other ideals' (M, p. 57), the highest personalities only 'in the struggle against the difficulties which life presents' (M, p. 55).

In his emphasis on the inevitability of conflict and tension in social life, Weber stands allied in moral temperament with his contemporary Sigmund Freud (Levine, 1981b). Both reject conceptions of a happy and harmonious social existence as illusory and disdain the impulse toward reconciliation and reunion as immature (Rieff, 1961, pp. xxii, 292). Both combine an unwavering commitment to scientific rationality with a keen awareness of its limited moral significance. Both aim to advance individual autonomy, to help individuals 'reach heightened levels of self-conscious free choice' (Levine, 1981b, p. 9) through a strenuous 'training in lucidity' (Rieff, 1961, p. xxii). At the center of their austere moral visions is not a new type of society but a new type of individual: one who harbors neither nostalgia for a golden past nor hope for a redeeming future but who, possessing a 'trained relentlessness in viewing the realities of life' (FMW, pp. 126–7), is able to measure up to the 'demands of the day' (FMW, p. 156).

NOTES TO CHAPTER 4

1 Others who have emphasized the moral impulse underlying Weber's scholarly work include Henrich (1952, pp. 105–31); Abramowski (1966, pp. 14–15, 161–85); Nelson (1965); Mitzman (1971); Mommsen (1974, esp. ch. 5); Schluchter (1979); and Levine (1981a, 1981b).

2 Strauss (1953, ch. 2), for example, identifies and criticizes the nihilistic implications of Weber's moral thought; Habermas (1970, pp. 63ff.; 1971, pp. 63–6; 1973, pp. 262ff.) criticizes what he calls Weber's 'decisionism'; and Levine (1981b) analyzes and criticizes Weber's one-sided emphasis on subjective freedom and subjective rationality and his corresponding neglect of 'agencies of moral socialization'.

3 The rootedness of Weber's moral thought in his philosophical anthropology has been stressed by Löwith (1982) and Henrich (1952, pp. 108ff).

4 This silence on the content of the truly human life has exposed Weber to the charge of nihilism—a charge developed most forcefully by Leo Strauss in

chapter 2 of *Natural Right and History* (1953); see also Factor and Turner (1979, p. 312).

5 See Fleischmann (1964) for an analysis of the influence of Nietzsche on Weber's social and moral thought.

6 This paradox is central not only to Weber's moral thought but also to his empirical work. In a passage about different paths of religious rationalization, for example, Weber notes that 'the various great rational and methodical [religious] ways of life rest on irrational presuppositions' (GAR, p. 253; FMW, p. 281).

7 By 'anthropological perspective' I mean the perspective of philosophical anthropology—broadly understood as the philosophical study of man.

8 For interpretations of Weber as a partisan of endangered Enlightenment values, see Henrich (1952, p. 122); Hughes (1958, p.334); and Bendix (1962, p. 9).

9 The account of moral reasoning given by some contemporary analytical moral philosophers is strikingly similar to that suggested by Weber:

> justificatory reasoning [according to R. M. Hare and other analytical philosophers] must always terminate with the assertion of some rule or principle for which no further reason can be given ... The terminus of justification is ... a choice unguided by criteria. Each individual implicitly or explicitly has to adopt his or her own first principles on the basis of such a choice. The utterance of any universal principle is in the end an expression of the preferences of an individual will and for that will its principles have and can have only such authority as it chooses to confer upon them by adopting them.

Alisdair Macintyre's *After Virtue* (1981), from which this passage is drawn (pp. 19–20), is among other things a sustained and intriguing criticism of this tradition in moral philosophy and thus—for the most part indirectly—of Weber's metaethical theory.

10 Criteria of rationality must be chosen even in the simplest choice situation—even when an unambiguous end is given and the task is to select the technically most rational means to this end. For what counts as the technically most rational solution depends on the standard of technical rationality that is adopted. Perhaps the standard is to realize the end in the shortest time, or with the lowest risk of serious injury or accident, or in a way that yields the most durable result. In any event, 'the various technically rational principles conflict with one another and a compromise can never be achieved from an "objective" standpoint but only from that of the concrete interests involved at the time' (M, p. 35).

11 Olafson (1967) interprets existentialist moral thought in terms of the 'progressive elaboration of the idea of moral autonomy and [the] substitution of this idea for the older conception of moral truth' (p. xiv). For an interesting discussion of the idea of autonomy in Weber's moral thought, see Levine (1981b).

12 Responsibility for one's ultimate value choices, meaning a clear, self-conscious awareness of their *logical implications*, must be distinguished from the feeling of responsibility for the *empirically foreseeable consequences* of one's actions that is required by the 'ethic of responsibility'. The former is a prerequisite of genuine moral autonomy for *all* individuals; the latter is the core of *one* of the two major ethical orientations distinguished by Weber—orientations between which the individual must simply choose.

13　For a nuanced analysis of Weber's conception of the relation between rationality and freedom, see Levine (1981a).

14　Weber describes the purely *zweckrational* orientation as follows. Instead of 'deciding between alternative and conflicting ends in terms of a rational orientation to a system of values', the actor may simply take his ends as 'given subjective wants and arrange them in a scale of consciously assessed relative urgency. He may then orient his action to this scale in such a way that they are satisfied as far as possible in order of urgency, as formulated in the principle of "marginal utility" ' (E&S, p. 26). While such purely *zweckrational* action is only a 'limiting case', this limiting case is increasingly approximated in reality (cf. n. 5 to Chapter 1 above).

15　The analogy is more than a superficial one. For while Weber, in a letter to Ferdinand Tönnies, describes himself as 'absolutely unmusical in religious matters' (Schluchter, 1979, p. 82, n. 44), his moral reflections nevertheless center on the quasi-religious problem of how man can redeem himself from the meaningless flux of a merely natural existence and achieve, if not a distinctively religious state of grace, at least the ennobling dignity of a truly human life.

Bibliography

(For Weber's works, see pp. vii–viii)

Abramowski, Günter, *Das Geschictsbild Max Webers* (Stuttgart: Klett, 1966).

Aron, Raymond, 'Max Weber and power-politics', in Stammer (1971), pp. 83–100.

Beetham, David, *Max Weber and the Theory of Modern Politics* (London: Allen & Unwin, 1974).

Bendix, Reinhard, *Max Weber: An Intellectual Portrait* (Garden City, NY: Doubleday, 1962).

Bruun, H. H., *Science, Values and Politics in Max Weber's Methodology* (Copenhagen: Munksgaard, 1972).

Camic, Charles, 'Charisma: its varieties, preconditions, and consequences', *Sociological Inquiry*, vol. 50, no. 1 (1980), pp. 5–23.

Collins, Randall, 'Weber's last theory of capitalism', *American Sociological Review*, vol. 45, no. 6 (1980), pp. 925–42.

Eisen, Arnold, 'The meanings and confusions of Weberian "rationality"', *British Journal of Sociology*, vol. 29, no. 1 (1978), pp. 57-70.

Factor, Regis, and Turner, Stephen, 'The limits of reason and some limitations of Weber's morality', *Human Studies*, vol. 2 (1979), pp. 301–34.

Fleischmann, Eugène, 'De Weber à Nietzsche', *Archives Européennes de Sociologie*, vol. 5 (1964), pp. 190–238.

Freud, Sigmund, *A General Introduction to Psychoanalysis* (New York: Pocket Books, 1953).

Freud, Sigmund, 'The Economic Problem in Masochism', in *General Psychological Theory* (New York: Collier, 1963), pp. 190–201.

Habermas, Jürgen, *Toward a Rational Society* (Boston: Beacon, 1970).

Habermas, Jürgen, 'Comments on Parsons' Paper on "Value-freedom and Objectivity"', in Stammer (1971), pp. 59–66.

Habermas, Jürgen, *Theory and Practice* (Boston: Beacon, 1973).

Henrich, Dieter, *Die Einheit der Wissenschaftslehre Max Webers* (Tübingen: Mohr, 1952).

Hughes, H. Stuart, *Consciousness and Society* (New York: Vintage, 1958).

Hume, David, *A Treatise of Human Nature* (Oxford: OUP, 1888).

Kalberg, Stephen, 'Max Weber's types of rationality', *American Journal of Sociology*, vol. 85, no. 5 (1980), pp. 1145–79.

Kant, Immanuel, *Groundwork of the Metaphysic of Morals* (New York: Harper & Row, 1964).

Kaufmann, Walter, 'Nietzsche', in *The Encyclopedia of Philosophy*, Vol. 5 (New York: Macmillan, 1967), pp. 504–14.

Levine, Donald N., 'Rationality and freedom: Weber and beyond', *Sociological Inquiry*, vol. 51, no. 1 (1981a), pp. 5–25.

Levine, Donald N., 'Freud, Weber, and modern rationales of conscience', unpublished paper (1981b), to be published in Levine (forthcoming).

Levine, Donald N., 'Subjective and objective rationality in Simmel's *Philosophy of Money*, Weber's account of rationalization, and Parsons' "theory of action" ', unpublished paper (1982), to be published in Levine (forthcoming).

Levine, Donald N., *The Flight from Ambiguity: Essays on Social and Cultural Theory* (Chicago: University of Chicago Press, forthcoming).

Löwith, Karl, *Max Weber and Karl Marx* (London: Allen & Unwin, 1982).

Macintyre, Alisdair, 'Existentialism', in *The Encyclopedia of Philosophy*, Vol. 3 (New York: Macmillan, 1967), pp. 147–54.

Macintyre, Alisdair, *After Virtue* (Notre Dame, Indiana: University of Notre Dame Press, 1981).

Mannheim, Karl, *Man and Society in an Age of Reconstruction* (New York: Harcourt, Brace & World, 1940).

Marcuse, Herbert, 'Industrialization and Capitalism', in Stammer (1971), pp. 133–51.

Mitzman, Arthur, *The Iron Cage* (New York: Grosset & Dunlap, 1971).

Mommsen, Wolfgang, 'Max Weber's political sociology and his philosophy of world history', *International Social Science Journal*, vol. 17, no. 1 (1965), pp. 23–45.

Mommsen, Wolfgang, *The Age of Bureaucracy* (Oxford: Blackwell, 1974).

Munson, Ronald (ed.), *Intervention and Reflection: Basic Issues in Medical Ethics* (Belmont, Calif.: Wadsworth, 1979).

Nelson, Benjamin, 'Dialogs across the Centuries', in *The Origins of Modern Consciousness*, ed. John Weiss (Detroit: Wayne State University Press, 1965), pp. 149–65.

Nelson, Benjamin, 'Comments on Herbert Marcuse's Paper on "Industrialization and Capitalism" ', in Stammer (1971), pp. 161–71.

Nelson, Benjamin, 'Weber's Protestant Ethic', in *Beyond the Classics?*, ed. Charles Y. Glock and Phillip E. Hammond (New York: Harper & Row, 1973), pp. 71–130.

Nelson, Benjamin, 'Max Weber's "Author's Introduction" (1920): a master clue to his main aims', *Sociological Inquiry*, vol. 44, no. 4 (1974), pp. 269–78.

Nelson, Benjamin, 'On Orient and Occident in Max Weber', *Social Research*, vol. 43, no. 1 (1976), pp. 114–29.

Neumann, Franz, *Behemoth: the Structure and Practice of National Socialism* (New York: Harper & Row, 1944).

Olafson, Frederick A., *Principles and Persons: an Ethical Interpretation of Existentialism* (Baltimore: Johns Hopkins, 1967).

Parsons, Talcott, 'Introduction', in *The Theory of Social and Economic Organization*, by Max Weber (New York: Oxford, 1947), pp. 3–86.

Parsons, Talcott, 'Introduction', in *The Sociology of Religion*, by Max Weber (Boston: Beacon, 1963), pp. xix–lxvii.

Parsons, Talcott, *The Structure of Social Action*, 2 Vols (New York: Free Press, 1968).

Parsons, Talcott, 'Value-freedom and Objectivity', in Stammer (1971), pp. 27–50.

Polanyi, Karl, *The Great Transformation* (Boston: Beacon, 1957).

Rieff, Philip, *Freud: the Mind of the Moralist* (Garden City, NY: Doubleday, 1961).

Schluchter, Wolfgang, 'The Paradox of Rationalization' and 'Value-neutrality and the Ethic of Responsibility', in *Max Weber's Vision of History*, by Guenther Roth and Wolfgang Schluchter (Berkeley: University of California Press, 1979), pp. 11–116.

Schluchter, Wolfgang, *The Rise of Western Rationalism: Max Weber's Developmental History* (Berkeley: University of California Press, 1981).

Simmel, Georg, *The Philosophy of Money* (London: Routledge & Kegan Paul, 1978).

Stammer, Otto, ed., *Max Weber and Sociology Today* (New York: Harper & Row, 1971).

Strauss, Leo, *Natural Right and History* (Chicago: University of Chicago Press, 1953).

Tenbruck, Friedrich H., 'The problem of thematic unity in the works of Max Weber', *British Journal of Sociology*, vol. 31, no. 3 (1980), pp. 316–51.

Index

Abramowski, G. 6, 112n
Aron, R. 111
asceticism 1–2, 22–9, 33; and rationalization of economic life, 23–4, 25–9
autonomy: as moral ideal 95, 100–1, 103, 112, 113n; threatened by rationalization 6, 22, 103–6, 110; *see also* freedom

Beetham, D. 46n, 48n
Bendix, R. 45n, 46n, 113n
Bruun, H. H. 87n
bureaucracy, bureaucratization 9, 13, 31, 46n; rationality of 20–2; as threat to freedom 3, 22, 34, 46n, 104 110–11

calculability of conduct 2, 4, 27, 31–2, 34, 36, 37–8, 52, 80, 86; in capitalist economy 3, 9, 10–15, 34, 41–3, 77–8; in bureaucracy 21, 34; in formalistic legal system 17–18, 34
Camic, C. 88n
capitalism 9, 32; rationality of 1–2, 4, 10–15, 45n; tension between formal and substantive rationality in 11–12, 15, 36, 38–43; and freedom 3, 34, 104, 110; development of 15, 23–4, 26–9
charisma 64–5, 88n
choice, non-rational 59, 67, 72, 74, 87, 98–102, 106–9, 113n
Collins, R. 45n
Comte, A. 3
control 2, 3, 10, 12–15, 31, 33–5, 37, 38, 40, 47n; *see also* self-control
conviction, ethic of (*Gesinnungsethik*) 78, 107–9

Darwin, C. 111
depersonalization, *see* impersonality
Diderto, D. 3
discipline 9, 12, 14–15, 27, 34, 40, 104
'Disenchantment' of the world 3, 31, 66, 80, 103
Durkheim, E. 44

Efficiency 21, 41–3, 46n
Eisen, A. 7n
enlightenment 3, 99, 113n
expertise *see* knowledge

Factor, R. 113n
Fleischmann, E. 113n
formalism 9; in law 16–20; in bureaucracy 20–2
freedom 3, 6, 17, 18–20, 22, 42, 46n. 93, 95, 104–6, 114n; *see also* autonomy
Freud, S. 55, 112

Habermas, J. 112n
Hare, R. M. 113n
Hegel, G. W. F. 3, 7n
Henrich, D. 112n, 113n
Hughes, H. S. 113n
Hume, D. 59, 91

impersonality 2, 28–9, 32–3, 37, 86; of capitalism, 3, 10, 11, 19, 32, 40–2, 77–8; of bureaucracy 9, 21–2, 33; of formalistic legal system 9, 19, 33; of ascetic ethic of vocation 24, 33
intellectualization 31–2, 66, 79

Kalberg, S. 4, 7n
Kant, I. 3, 7n, 100, 105
Kaufmann, W. 98
knowledge 2, 3, 9, 13, 21–2, 30–2, 33–4, 37; *see also* science

Levine, D. 1, 3, 7n, 46n, 60n, 101, 112, 112n, 113n, 114n
Löwith, K. 44, 48n, 91, 106, 112, 112n
Luther, M. 89n

Macintyre, A. 100, 113n
Marcuse, H. 47n, 48n
Marx, K. 9, 13, 44, 88n
meaning and meaninglessness 31, 62–8, 76, 80–2, 87n, 92, 94, 103
Merton, R. K. 88n, 90n
Mitzman, A. 88n, 90n, 111, 112n

Mommsen, W. 45n, 46n, 48n, 104, 112n
Montesquieu 3
Munson, R. 52

Nelson, B. 8, 44, 45n, 46n, 111, 112n
Neumann, F. 88n
Nietzsche, F. 98, 101, 111
nihilism 112n

Olafson, F. 101, 113n

Parsons, T. 45n, 46n, 48n
personality 62–3, 95, 105, 110; rationalization of 24, 27, 29; as moral ideal 22, 63, 96–100
Plato 44
Polanyi, K. 38
predictability, 12, 15, 17, 34; *see also* calculability
Protestant ethic, *see* asceticism

rationalism, modern Western: uniqueness of 2, 8–35, 37–8, 43–4; as morally and politically problematic 3–4, 6–7, 10, 38–44; ambivalent attitude of Weber towards 3, 7, 11, 109–110
rationality; as neutral analytical concept 10–11, 25, 36–7, 42, 47n, 55; as relational concept 4, 35–6; meaning(s) of 1–2, 8, 29–30, 46–47n, 49–50, 77–8, 86–7; limits of 5, 40, 44–5, 49, 52, 63–60, 61, 77–8, 87, 98–101; formal and substantive rationality 4, 10, 11–12, 15, 18, 19–20, 22, 30, 35–45, 47n, 48n, 52, 78, 86–7, 111; technical rationality 5, 33–4, 37–8, 56–9; moral rationality 98–103; subjective rationality 5, 11, 12, 46n, 50, 51, 53–7; objective rationality 5, 12, 50, 53–60, 60n; objectified rationality 9, 11, 23, 46n, 51, 60n; instrumental rationality, *see Zweckrationalität*; value-rationality, *see Wertrationalität*
rationalization, process(es) of 2–4, 8, 9, 13–14, 15, 18, 22, 23, 26–7, 29, 30, 32, 50–1, 52, 60n, 65–6, 74–5, 102–4; in the economic sphere 15, 23–9; in the legal sphere 16–17; in the administrative sphere 13, 22; in the

religious sphere 23–9, 47n, 75–8, 89n; in the scientific and technical sphere 13–14, 30–1; in the sphere of intellectual culture 31, 66, 79–82; in the aesthetic sphere, 78–9; in the erotic sphere, 78
relativism, ethical 5–6, 69
responsibility, ethic of 7, 70–1, 106–110, 113n
Rieff, P. 112n

Schluchter, W. 45n, 46n, 82, 87n, 89n, 107, 110, 111, 112n, 114n
science, 4, 33–4, 36, 44–5, 66–7, 69, 110; and the development of Western rationalism 3, 13–14, 30–1; and the development of capitalism 12, 13; and the 'disenchantment of the world' 3, 31, 66, 80; and rational action 56–69, *see also* knowledge
self-control, 9, 24, 25, 35, 37; *see also* control
Simmel, G. 3, 7n, 46n, 48n
Socialism, 38, 43, 48n
Socrates, 79, 80, 84
Strauss, L. 87n, 112n

Tenbruck, F. 45n
Tönnies, F. 3, 7n, 114n
traditionalism: overcoming of 13–14, 23, 27; as obstacle to rationalization 27
Turner, S. *see* Factor, R.

value conflict 5–6, 60, 61–87
value spheres 6; defined, 69; conflict among 72–87; 'autonomy' (*Eigengesetzlichkeit*) of 74–5, 83–5; ambiguity of concept 85
value-orientations 5–6, 84; defined 62–3; conflict among 65–9; as subjective 66–7, 72–3
Voltaire, 3

Wertrationalität (value-rationality) 49–50, 51–5, 77–8, 85–7, 92, 106; 108–9

zweckrationalität (instrumental rationality) 6, 10, 32, 45n, 49, 50, 51–5, 60n, 77–8, 85–7, 90n, 92, 104–6, 108–11, 114n